Penguin Books
Puckoon

Spike Milligan was born at Ahmednagar in
India in 1919. He received his first education
in a tent in the Hyderabad Sindh desert and
graduated from there through a series of
Roman Catholic schools in India and England
to the Lewisham Polytechnic. Always
something of a playboy, he then plunged into
the world of Show Business, seduced by his
first stage appearance, at the age of eight, in
the nativity play of his Poona convent school.
He began his career as a band musician but has
since become famous as a humorous script
writer and actor both in films and broadcasting.
He was one of the main figures in and behind
the infamous Goon Show. Among the films
he has appeared in are: *Suspect, Invasion,
Postman's Knock* and *Milligan at Large*. Apart
from *Puckoon* Spike Milligan has also published
The Little Potboiler, Silly Verse for Kids (a Puffin
Book), *Dustbin of Milligan, A Book of Bits,
The Bed-Sitting Room* (a play), *The Bald Twit
Lion, A Book of Milliganimals* (also in
Puffins) and *Adolf Hitler – My Part in His Downfall*
(published in Penguins). His latest publication is
a collection of poems, *Small Dreams of a Scorpion*,
which is also available in Penguins. He is married,
has three children and lives in London.

Spike Milligan
Puckoon

Penguin Books

Penguin Books Ltd, Harmondsworth,
Middlesex, England
Penguin Books Australia Ltd, Ringwood,
Victoria, Australia
Penguin Books Canada Ltd, 41 Steelcase Road West,
Markham, Ontario, Canada

First published by Anthony Blond 1963
Published in Penguin Books 1965
Reprinted 1965, 1966, 1967, 1968, 1969, 1970, 1971,
1972, 1973 (twice), 1974 (twice)

Made and printed in Great Britain by
Cox & Wyman Ltd,
London, Reading and Fakenham
Set in Monotype Baskerville

Foreword

This damn book nearly drove me mad. I
started it in 1958 and doodled with it for 4
years. I don't think I could go through it all
again, therefore, as this will be my first and
last novel, I would like to thank those who
helped me get it finished. First I want to
thank me, then Paddy my wife; without her,
for certain reasons, this book would never
have been completed. I also thank my
family for eternal encouragement, Harry
Edgington my old army pal, who cheered me
up when I was down, Gordon Lansborough
who told me the novel was funny when I
thought it wasn't, my three children, Laura,
Sean and Sile, who think I'm good '*all* the
time'. To Patrick Ford, the man who sold
me good wine, Mrs Jolly who typed it, and
the human race for being the butt of all my
jokes.

SPIKE MILLIGAN,
S.S. *Canberra*,
Indian Ocean.

Chapter One

Several and a half metric miles North East of Sligo, split by a cascading stream, her body on earth, her feet in water, dwells the microcephalic community of Puckoon. This June of a Morning, the whole village awoke to an unexpected burst of hot weather. Saffron coloured in the bleach early sky, the sun blistered down, cracking walls and curling the brims of the old men's winter-damp hats; warm-bum biddies circulated air in their nethers, flapping their skirts and easing their drawers. Joyous voiced children fought for turns at the iron pump, their giggling white bodies splashing in the cool water from its maternal maw; bone-dreaming dogs steamed on the pavements and pussy cats lay, bellies upwards, drinking the gold effulgent warmth through their fur; leather-faced fishcatchers puzzled at the coarse Atlantic now flat and stunned by its own salt hot inertia. Shimmering black and still, it lay at the mercy of stone-throwing boys; the bowmen of the sands took respite from the endless cavalry charges of the sea. Nearby, Castle Hill groaned under the weight of its timeless ruins, while the distant mountains came and went in the mid-morning haze. Old Danny Conlon was already setting up the evening edition with ink-tinted fingers, 'Hottest Day in Living Memory', it took something like that to get the Pope off the front page; so lay Puckoon caught by summer in her winter thrawl, as she lay thus dreaming 'twixt land and sea, all was light, and like a golden finger the morning was writ upon the scene.

Gleaming off-white at the foot of Castle Hill were the puzzled crumbling faces of the old peat cutters' cottages, their glass eyes now dimmed with cataracts of neglect and dirt. The peat had run out thirty years ago and the peat cutters had run out not long after; some went to America, the rest stayed behind and hit each other with loaded sticks but it never really caught on and they dispersed. The cottages had been condemned as unfit to live in except during thunderstorms and depressions. The year after 'the troubles', the Irish Free State Government had bequeathed the cottages to those who had helped rid 'Houly Ireland' of the English, the Tans and for that matter, anybody. One such beneficiary was the Dan Milligan, son of a famous paternity order. With a roof over his head he had ceased work, living off his pension and his wits, both hopelessly inadequate. This sun-barbed morning the Milligan lay full length on the grass, head against the wall, his eyes lost in the shadow of his cap. His thoughts, few that they were, lay silent in the privacy of his head. Across the road, through a gap in the hedge, Milligan observed a nobbly brown dog snoozed down on the grass verge, now it was one of those creatures that dozes with eyes half open, but, to Milligan, a Catholic, it would appear the animal was giving him a long sensual erotic stare: Milligan moved uneasily in his holy Catholic trousers. 'I wonder if he's trying to hypnotize me,' he thought, avoiding the creature's eyes. 'You can't be too care-

8

ful dese days wid all dem patent medicines about!'

In an attempt to break the white man's supremacy, Paul Robeson had once remarked 'All handsome men are slightly sunburned'. Milligan was no exception, he had also said it. He sat in the half upright. 'I tink,' he reflected, 'I tink I'll bronze me limbs.' He rolled his trousers kneewards revealing the like of two thin white hairy affairs of the leg variety. He eyed them with obvious dissatisfaction. After examining them he spoke out aloud. 'Holy God! Wot are dese den? Eh?' He looked around for an answer. 'Wot are dey?' he repeated angrily.

'Legs.'

'Legs? LEGS? Whose legs?'

'Yours.'

'Mine? And who are you?'

'The Author.'

'Author? Author? Did you write these legs?'

'Yes.'

'Well, I don't like dem. I don't like 'em at all at all. I could ha' writted better legs meself. Did you write your legs?'

'No.'

'Ahhh. *Sooo*! You got some one else to write your legs, some one who's a good leg writer and den you write dis pair of crappy old legs fer me, well mister, it's not good enough.'

'I'll try and develop them with the plot.'

'It's a dia-bo-likal liberty lettin' an untrained leg writer loose on an unsuspectin' human bean like me.'

It was a Dublin accent charged with theatrical innuendo; like all Irish he could make Good Morning sound like a declaration of war – which it usually was.

'Now, listen Milligan, I'll grant you a word wish. If you ever find yourself in trouble just shout "Squrrox".'

'Squrrox?'

'Squrrox.'

'Alrite alrite, Squorrox, I'll remember dat. Squorrox,' he repeated, 'Right, Squorrox.'

He lay back, the sun grew on. 'I must admit you write nice weather, mister.' He held one arm up to the sky and eyed the frayed cuffs of a once-upon-a-time suit.

'It's goin' home at last, still a suit can't last for ever.' But on reflection he remembered it had.

The shoulders were padded like angled flight decks, the trouser seat hung a foot below the crutch and the twenty-eight inch bottoms flapped round his legs like curtains. He shook his head sadly.

'Ahh, they don't make suits like dis any more, I suppose the age of Beau Brummel is dead.'

He recalled the day he'd bought it. The bride-to-be waiting at the church while he, the groom, was still at home, standing naked in front of a mirror, a top hat angled jauntily on his head. 'By Gor, she's getting value for money,' he said.

'Hurry up, Dan lad,' his father was saying, 'you're late, and you can't get married in that nude.'

'And why not?' said Milligan, admiring his honeymoon appendages, 'Adam and Eve done it and look at the fine honeymoon dey had.'

'Thank God,' said the old man, 'dere were no press photographers at dat weddin', or the Houly Bible would ha' been banned in Ireland for ever, perhaps longer.'

His two brothers had arrived with the suit just in time to get him to the wedding. He never forgave them, standing at the altar with two dirty great cut price tickets hangin' down his back. It was all so long ago. Suits were cheap in dem days, this one only cost a poun' ten shillin'. Prices must have gone up since then. 'Why, it must be nearly two thousand pounds for a suit dese days,' he reflected.

Kersploosh! A bucket of evil-smelling slops hit him square in his sleeping face.

'And there's more where that came from, you lazy bugger.'

The owner of the voice stepped from the cottage into the white sunlight.

'God forgive yez for dat,' spluttered the now reeking Milligan. 'Me hat! Look at me hat.'

With nostrils and legs akimbo, she towered over him like some human Yggdrasill, blotting out the sun.

'Owwwwwwwwww!' shrieked the Milligan as she kicked the sole of his boot.

'If you don't get some work soon I'll – ' she made the sign of slow manual strangulation. Milligan noticed that of a sudden there were no birds in the sky and the brown dog had fled.

'Owwww!' She kicked his other boot.

'Darling,' he whined – 'you know full well dere's no work round dese parts,' and he pointed as far as the fence.

'Poor Father Rudden is *still* looking for someone to

cut the church grass, I'm going in for five minutes, if you're still here when I come out in half an hour –'.

'Owwww!' She kicked his boot again. Like an Amen the cottage door slammed after her. All the world went quiet.

'Holy God! Who in the blazes was *dat*?'

'That's your darling little wife.'

'Wife? Wife?' Agony swept across his face. 'Man alive, I thought it was a *man*. Good God, did you see dem arms? Jack Dempsey would be world champion again if he could get 'em. What kind of a writer are you? First me legs, and now this great hairy creature!'

'Don't worry, Milligan, I'll see you come out of this alive.'

'Alive?' He sat bolt upright. 'Holy Christ! Is dis a murder mystery? If so include me out, Mister. I'm a Catlick, a Holy Roman Catlick.' He listened towards the cottage. 'I better get after dat job.' He stood up, yawned, stretched, farted and lay down again. 'No need to rush at it,' he yawned. Kersploosh!! A bucket of evil-smelling slops hit him square in his face.

'I'm gettin' out of dis chapter, it's too bloody unlucky for me.'

Chapter Two

The Dan Milligan cycled tremendously towards the Church of St Theresa of the Little Flowers. Since leaving the area known as his wife he had brightened up a little. 'Man alive! The *size* of her though, she's a danger to shipping, I mean, every time I put me key in the front door I'll wonder what I'm lettin' meself in for.' Away down a lumpy road he pedalled, his right trouser leg being substantially chewed to pulp in the chain. His voice was raised in that high nasal Irish tenor, known and hated the world over.

'Ohhhhhhhhhhhhhhh IIIIIIIIIIIIII
         Once knew a judy in Dubleen Town
         Her eyes were blue and her hair was brown,
         One night on the grass I got her down
         And I . . .'

The rest of the words were lost to view as he turned a bend in the road. Farther along, from an overhanging branch, a pure-blooded Irish crow watched the Milligan approach. It also watched him hit the pothole, leave the bike, strike the ground, clutch the shin, scream the agony, swear the word. 'Caw!' said the crow. 'Balls!' said the Milligan. Peering intently from behind a wall was something that Milligan could only hope was a face. The fact that it was hanging from a hat gave credulity to his belief.

'Are you all right, Milligan?' said the face in the hat.

'Oh ho!' Milligan's voice showed recognition. 'It's Murphy. Tell me, why are you wearing dat terrible lookin' trilby?'

'We sold der hat stand, an' dere's no place ter hang it.' Murphy's face was a replica of the King Edwards he grew. He did in fact look like King Edward the Seventh. He also resembled King Edward the Third, Fifth and Second, making a grand total of King Edward the Seventeenth. He had a mobile face, that is, he always took it with him. His nose was what the French call retroussé, or as we say, like a pig; his nostrils were so acutely angled, in stormy weather the rain got in and forced him indoors. His eyebrows grew from his head like Giant Coypu rats, but dear friends, when you and I talk of eyebrows, we know not what eyebrows be until we come face to face with the *Murphy's* eyebrows! The man's head was a veritable plague of eyebrows, black, grey, brown and red they grew, thick as thieves. They covered two-thirds of his skull, both his temples and the entire bridge of his nose. In dry weather they bristled from his head like the spears of an avenging army and careless flies were impaled by the score. In winter they glistened with hoar-frost and steamed by the fire. When wet they hung down over his eyes and he was put to shaking himself like a Cocker Spaniel before he could proceed. For all their size dose eyebrows were as mobile as piglets, and in moments of acute agitation had been seen as far south as his chin. At the first sight of Milligan they had wagged up and down, agitati ma non troppo. As he spoke they both began to revolve round his head at speed.

MURPHY

'I heeerd a crash,' said Murphy. 'I examined meself, and I knew it wasn't me.'

'It was me,' said Milligan. 'I felled off me bi-cycle. Tank heaven the ground broke me fall.'

'Oh yes, it's very handy like dat,' said Murphy, settling his arms along the wall.

'Oh dear, dear!' said Milligan, getting to his feet. 'I've scratched all the paint off the toe of me boot.'

'Is dat right den, you paint yer boots?'

'True, it's the most economical way. Sometimes I paints 'em brown, when I had enough o' dat I paints 'em black again. Dat way people tink you got more than one pair, see? Once when I played the cricket I painted 'em white, you should try dat.'

'Oh no,' said Murphy solemnly. 'Oh no, I don't like inteferring wid nature. Der natural colour of boots is black as God ordained, any udder colour and a man is askin' fer trouble.'

'Oh, and what I may ask is wrong wid brown boots?'

'How do I know? I never had a pair.'

'Take my tip, Murphy, you got to move wid der times man. The rich people in Dublin are all wearin' the brown boots; when scientists spend a lifetime inventin' a thing like the brown boots, we should take advantage of the fact.'

'No, thank you,' said Murphy's eyebrows, 'I'll stick along wid the inventor of the black boots. After all they don't show the dirt.'

'Dat's my argument, black don't show the dirt, brown ones don't show the mud and a good pair of green boots won't show the grass.'

'By Gor', you got something dere,' said the Murphy. 'But wait, when you was wearing dem white boots, what didn't dey show?'

'They didn't show me feet,' said Milligan, throwing himself on to the bike and crashing down on the other side.

'Caw!' said the crow.

'BALLS!' said Milligan. 'I'll be on me way.' He remounted and pedalled off.

'No, stay and have a little more chat,' called Murphy across the widening gap. 'Parts round here are lonely and sparse populated.'

'Well it's not for the want of you tryin',' came the fading reply.

The day brewed hotter now, it was coming noon. The hedgerows hummed with small things that buzzed and bumbled in the near heat. From the cool woods came a babel of chirruping birds. The greenacious daisy-spattled fields spread out before Milligan, the bayonets of grass shining bravely in the sun, above him the sky was an exaltation of larks. Slowfully Milligan pedalled on his way. Great billy bollers of perspiration were running down his knees knose and kneck, the torrents ran down his shins into his boots where they escaped through the lace holes as steam. 'Now,' thought the Milligan, 'why are me legs goin' round and round? eh? I don't tink it's me doin' it, in fact, if I had me way dey wouldn't be doin' it at all. But dere dey are goin' round and round; what den was der drivin' force behind dose legs? Me wife! *That's* what's drivin' 'em round and round, dat's the truth, dese legs are terrified of me wife, terrified of bein' kicked in the soles of the feet again.' It was a disgrace how a fine mind like his should be taken along by a pair of terrified legs. If only his mind had a pair of legs of its own they'd be back at the cottage being bronzed in the Celtic sun.

The Milligan had suffered from his legs terribly. During the war in Italy. While his mind was full of great heroisms under shell fire, his legs were carrying the idea, at speed, in the opposite direction. The Battery Major had not understood.

'Gunner Milligan? You have been acting like a coward.'

'No sir, not true. I'm a hero wid coward's legs, I'm a hero from the waist up.'

'Silence! Why did you leave your post?'

'It had woodworm in it, sir, the roof of the trench was falling in.'

'Silence! You acted like a coward!'

'I wasn't acting sir!'

'I could have you shot!'

'Shot? Why didn't they shoot me in peacetime? I was still the same coward.'

'Men like you are a waste of time in war. Understand?'

'Oh? Well den! Men like *you* are a waste of time in peace.'

'Silence when you speak to an officer,' shouted the Sgt. Major at Milligan's neck.

All his arguments were of no avail in the face of military authority. He was court martialled, surrounded by clanking top brass who were not cowards and therefore biased.

'I may be a coward, I'm not denying dat sir,' Milligan told the prosecution..'But you can't really *blame* me for being a coward. If I am, then you might as well hold me responsible for the shape of me nose, the colour of me hair and the size of me feet.'

'Gunner Milligan,' Captain Martin stroked a cavalry moustache on an infantry face. 'Gunner Milligan,' he said. 'Your personal evaluations of cowardice do not concern the court. To refresh your memory I will read the precise military definition of the word.'

He took a book of King's Regulations, opened a marked page and read 'Cowardice'. Here he paused and gave Milligan a look.

He continued: 'Defection in the face of the enemy. Running away.'

'I was not running away sir, I was retreating.'

'The whole of your Regiment were advancing, and you decided to retreat?'

'Isn't dat what you calls personal initiative?'

'Your action might have caused your comrades to panic and retreat.'

'Oh, I see! One man retreating is called running away, but a whole Regiment running away is called a retreat? I demand to be tried by cowards!'

A light, commissioned-ranks-only laugh passed around the court. But this was no laughing matter. These lunatics could have him shot.

'Have you anything further to add?' asked Captain Martin.

'Yes,' said Milligan. 'Plenty. For one ting I had no desire to partake in dis war. I was dragged in. I warned the Medical Officer, I told him I was a coward, and he marked me A.1. for Active Service. I gave everyone fair warning! I told me Battery Major before it started, I even wrote to Field Marshal Montgomery. Yes, I warned everybody, and now you're all acting surprised?'

Even as Milligan spoke his mind, three non-cowardly judges made a mental note of Guilty.

'Is that all?' queried Martin with all the assurance of a conviction. Milligan nodded. What was the use? After all, if Albert Einstein stood for a thousand years in front of fifty monkeys explaining the theory of relativity, at the end, they'd still be just monkeys.

Anyhow it was all over now, but he still had these cowardly legs which, he observed, were still going round and round. 'Oh dear, dis weather, I niver knowed it so hot.' It felt as though he could have grabbed a handful of air and squeezed the sweat out of it. 'I wonder,' he mused, 'how long can I go on losin' me body fluids at dis rate before I'm struck down with the dehydration? Ha ha! The answer to me problems,' he said, gleefully drawing level with the front door of the 'Holy Drunkard' pub.

'Hello! Hi-lee, Ho-la, Hup-la!' he shouted through the letter box.

Upstairs, a window flew up like a gun port, and a pig-of-a-face stuck itself out.

'What do you want, Milligan?' said the pig-of-a-face. Milligan doffed his cap.

'Ah, Missis O'Toole, you're looking more lovely

dan ever. Is there any chance of a cool libation for a tirsty traveller?'

'Piss off!' said the lovely Mrs O'Toole.

'Oh what a witty tongue you have today,' said Milligan, gallant in defeat. Well, he thought, you can fool some of the people all the time and all the people some of the time, which is just long enough to be President of the United States, and on that useless profundity, Milligan himself pedalled on, himself, himself.

'Caw!' said a crow.

'Balls!' said Milligan.

Father Patrick Rudden paused as he trod the gravel path of the church drive. He ran his 'kerchief round the inside of his holy clerical collar. Then he walked slowly to the grave of the late Miss Griselda Strains and pontifically lowered his ecclesiastical rump on to the worn slab, muttering a silent apology to the departed lady, but reflecting, it wouldn't be the first time she'd had a man on top of her, least of all one who apologized as he did. He was a tall handsome man touching fifty, but didn't appear to be speeding. His stiff white hair was yellowed with frequent applications of anointment oil. The width of neck and shoulder suggested a rugby player, the broken nose confirmed it. Which shows how wrong you can be as he never played the game in his life. The clock in the church tower said 4.32, as it had done for three hundred years. It was right once a day and that was better than no clock at all. How old the church was no-one knew. It was, like Mary Brannigan's black baby, a mystery. Written records went back to 1530. The only *real* clue was the discovery of a dead skeleton under the ante-chapel. Archaeologists from Dublin had got wind of it and come racing up in a lorry filled with little digging men, instruments and sandwiches.

'It's the bones of an Ionian monk,' said one grey professor. For weeks they took photos of the dear monk. They measured his skull, his shins, his dear elbows; they took scrapings from his pelvis, they took a plaster cast of the dear fellow's teeth, they dusted him with resin and preserving powders and finally the professors had all agreed, the Monk was one thousand five hundred years old. 'Which accounts for him being dead,' said the priest, and that was that.

Money! That was the trouble. Money! The parish was spiritually solvent but financially bankrupt. Money! The Lord will provide, but to date he was behind with his payments. Money! Father Rudden had tried everything to raise funds, he even went to the bank. 'Don't be a fool, Father!' said the manager, 'Put that gun down.' Money! There was the occasion he'd promised to make fire to fall from heaven. The church had been packed. At the psychological moment the priest had mounted the pulpit and called loudly 'I command fire to fall from heaven!' A painful silence followed. The priest seemed uneasy. He repeated his invocation much louder, 'I COMMAND FIRE TO FALL FROM HEAVEN!' The sibilant voice of the verger came wafting hysterically from the loft. 'Just a minute, Father, the cat's pissed on the matches!'

It had been a black day for the church. Money! That was the trouble. His own shoes were so worn he knew every pebble in the church drive by touch. He poked a little gold nut of cheap tobacco into his pipe. As he drew smoke he looked at the honeyed stone of St Theresa, the church he had pastored for thirty years. A pair of nesting doves flew from the ivy on the tower. It was pretty quiet around here. There had been a little excitement during the insurgence; the Sinn Fein had held all their meetings in the bell tower and in consequence were all stone deaf. The priest didn't like bloodshed, after all we only have a limited amount, but what was he to do?

Freedom! The word had been burning through the land for nearly four hundred years. The Irish had won battles for everyone but themselves; now the fever of liberty was at the high peak of delirium, common men were incensed by injustice; now the talk was over and the guns were speaking. Father Rudden had thrown in his lot with 'the lads' and had harboured gunmen on the run. They had won but alas, even then, Ulster had come out against the union. For months since the armistice, dozens of little semi-important men with theodolites and creased trousers, were running in all directions in a frenzy of mensuration, threats and rock-throwing, all trying to agree the new border.

The sound of a male bicycle frame drew the priest's attention. There coming up the drive was the worst Catholic since Genghis Khan.

'Ah, top of the morning to yez, Father,' Milligan said dismounting.

'Well, well, Dan Milligan.' There was surprise and

23

pleasure in the priest's voice. 'Tell me, Dan, what are you doing so far from your dear bed?'

'I'm feeling much better, Father.'

'Oh? You been ill then?'

'No, but I'm feeling much better now dan I felt before.'

There was a short pause, then a longer one, but so close were they together, you couldn't tell the difference.

'It's unexpectedly hot fer dis time of the year, Father.'

'Very hot, Milligan. Almost hot enough to burn a man's conscience, eh?'

'Ha ha, yes, Father,' he laughed weakly, his eyes two revelations of guilt.

'When did you last come to church, Milligan?'

'Oh, er, I forget – but I got it on me Baptismal certificate.'

The priest gave Milligan a long meaning stare which Milligan did not know the meaning of. Then the Milligan, still holding his bike, sat down next to the priest. 'By Gor Father, wot you tink of dis weather?'

'Oh, it's hot all right,' said Father Rudden relighting his pipe. Producing a small clay decoy pipe, Milligan started to pat his empty pockets. 'Here,' said the priest, throwing him his tobacco pouch.

'Oh tank you Father, an unexpected little treat.'

Together the two men sat in silence; sometimes they stood in silence which after all is sitting in silence only higher up. An occasional signal of smoke escaped from the bowl and scurried towards heaven. 'Now Milligan,' the priest eventually said, 'what is the purpose of this visit?' Milligan knew that this was, as the Spaniards say, '*El Momento de la Verdad*', mind you, he didn't think it in Spanish, but if he had, that's what it would have looked like.

'Well Father,' he began, puffing to a match, 'well, I – "puff-puff-puff" – I come to see – "puff-puff" – if dis grass cuttin' – job – "puff-puff" – is still goin'.'

The inquiry shook the priest into stunned silence. In that brief moment the Milligan leaped on to his bike with a 'Ah well, so the job's gone, good-bye.' The priest recovered quickly, restraining Milligan by the seat of the trousers.

'Oh, steady Father,' gasped Milligan, 'dem's more then me trousers yer clutchin'.'

'Sorry, Milligan,' said the priest, releasing his grip. 'We celibates are inclined to forget them parts.' 'Well you can forget mine fer a start,' thought Milligan. Why in God's name did men have to have such tender genitals. He had asked his grandfather that question. 'Don't worry 'bout yer old genitals lad,' said the old man, 'they'll stand up fer themselves.'

What about that terrible, terrible evening so long ago? Dan Milligan was seventeen, he had arrived for his first date with Mary Nolan. Her father had ushered him into the parlour with a forked vermin stick. Alone in the room with him was Mary's youngest brother, a little toddler of four. The little fellow carried in his hand such an innocent thing as a clay lion, but this, plus momentum, and brought unexpectedly into violent contact with Milligan's testicles, caused him to writhe and scream with pain; at which moment the radiant Mary chose to enter the room. To be caught clutching himself so was too much for the sensitive Dan. With only the whites of his eyes showing, he disguised his convulsions as a macabre Highland fling. Cross-eyed, bent double and screaming 'Och aye!' he danced from the room and she never saw him again. For many years after, young Dan Milligan wore an outsized cricketer's protective cup; during the mixed bathing season, many ladies made his acquaintance, only to be disappointed later.

'Yes, there's plenty of work to be done, Dan,' the priest was saying. He led Milligan to the gardener's hut. A small wood plank shed tucked in a cluster of cool elms. 'Michael Collins himself hid in here from the Tans,' said the priest proudly as he opened the door.

'Did he ever cut the grass?'

'No, but once, when the English was after him he set fire to it. What a blaze! Twenty courtin' couples nearly burnt to death! Them's the tools.' The priest pointed to four sentinel scythes standing in the corner like steel flamingoes.

'Ooh!' Milligan backed away. 'They look awful heavy, Father. Would you like ter lift one to see if me fears are well founded?'

'Saints alive, Milligan, there's no weight in 'em at all, man,' said the priest, lifting one and making long sweeping strokes. 'See? No weight in 'em at all,' he repeated, holding his groin for suspected rupture. He stood at the door and pointed out. 'You can start against that wall there and work inwards. If only I was younger.'

So saying the priest made off up the path. As he did, Milligan thought he heard suppressed laughter coming from the holy man. Carefully Milligan folded his jacket and cap and placed them on the roots of a flowering oak. He turned and faced the ocean of tall waving grass. His unshaven face took on that worried look of responsibility. Spitting in his hands he took hold of the instrument. Placing his feet apart he threw the scythe behind him, then, with a cry of 'Hi ayeee! Hoo! Hup-la!' he let go with a mighteous low curling chop; it started way behind him but, never a man of foresight, so great was the initial momentum, by the time the scythe had travelled ninety degrees it was beyond his control. All he could do was hang on; the great blade flashed past his white terrified face disappearing behind his back, taking both of his arms out of sight and sockets, at the same time corkscrewing his legs which gave off an agonized crackling sound from his knees. For a brief poetic moment he stayed twisted and poised, then fell sideways like a felled ox. 'Must be nearly lunch time,' he thought as he hit the ground. The Lord said: 'Six days shalt thou labour and on the seventh thou shalt rest.' He hadn't reckoned wid the unions. Forty-eight hours a week shalt thou labour and on the seventh thou shalt get double time. Ha. It was more profitable to be in the unions.

As Milligan laboured unevenly through the afternoon, long overgrown tombstones came to light,

R.I.P.
Tom Conlon O'Rourke.
Not Dead, just Sleeping.

'He's not kiddin' anyone but himself,' Milligan chuckled irreverently. What was all dis dyin' about, anyhow? It was a strange and mysterious thing, no matter how you looked at it. 'I wonder what heaven is really like? Must be pretty crowded by now, it's been goin' a long time.' Did they have good lunches? Pity dere was so little information. Now, if there was more brochures on the place, more people might be interested in going dere. *Dat's* what the church needed, a good Public Relations man. 'Come to heaven where it's real cool.' 'Come to heaven and enjoy the rest.' 'Come to heaven where old friends meet, book now to avoid disappointment!' Little catch phrases like dat would do the place a power of good. Mind you, dere were other questions, like did people come back to earth after they die, like them Buddhists say.

In dat religion you got to come back as an animal. Mmm, a cat! Dat's the best animal to come back as, sleep all day, independent, ha! that was the life, stretched out in front of a fire, but no, Oh hell, they might give me that terrible cat operation, no no I forgot about that. Come to think of it, who the hell wants to come back again anyhow? Now, honest, how many people in life have had a good enough time to come back? Of course if you could come back as a woman you could see the other side of life? By gor, dat would be an experience, suppose you wakes up one morning and finds you're a woman? What would he do? Go for a walk and see what happens. Oh yes, all this dyin' was a funny business, still, it was better to believe in God than not. You certainly couldn't believe in men. Bernard Shaw said 'Every man over forty is a scoundrel', ha ha ha, Milligan laughed aloud, 'Every one round dese parts is a scoundrel at sixteen!' Bernard Shaw, dere was a great man, the Irish Noel Coward. A tiny insect with wings hovered stock still in front of Milligan's face. 'I wonder if he's tryin' to hypnotize me,' he thought, waving the creature away.

The sun bled its scarlet way to the horizon and the skies nodded into evening. The birds flew to their secret somewheres, and bats grew restless at the coming of night. Milligan puzzled at the church clock. 4.32? Good heavens, it gets dark early round here.

'How are you getting on then, Dan?'

At the sound of the priest's voice, Milligan put on a brief energetic display of hoeing. The priest blew his nose. 'Farnnnn – farnnnnnnnn,' it went, in a deep melodious E♭. 'I think you've done enough for today, it's nearly seven.'

'Seven?' Milligan cursed in his head. 'Trust me to work to a bloody stopped clock!'

'You mustn't kill yerself, Milligan.'

'I'm in the right place if I do.'

They both laughed.

A cool breeze blew in from the Atlantic, fetching the smell of airborne waves. The first ectoplasms of evening mist were forming over the river. Here and there fishes mouthed an O at the still surface. The Angelus rang out its iron prayer. Murphy, out in his fields, dropped his hoe and joined hands in prayer. 'The Angel of the Lord declared unto Mary.'

The near Godless Milligan trundled his bike towards the Holy Drinker,

'IIIIIII
>
> Once knew a Judy in Dubleen town
> Her eyes were blue and her hair was brown
> One night on the grass I got her downnnn
> and the . . .'

The rest of the words were lost to view as the song turned a bend* in the road.

'I wonder if I'll see him again,' pondered Father Rudden. For that reason he had refrained from paying Milligan by the day.

*This was a different bend to the previous one. S.M.

Chapter Three

The pub door flew in and a fast stream of silent drinkers moved into position. The air was immediately machine-gunned with a rapid series of orders – 'Guinness – Whiskey – Stout – Gin – Beer – Rum – Port – Beer – Stout – Stout –'. There followed a silence as the day's troubles were washed away with great liver-crippling draughts of alcohol. Stock still they stood, waiting the warming glow that makes us acceptable to all men and vice versa. The first one to feel a powerful benefit was blind George Devine, a thin white El Greco figure with two sightless sockets.

'Good evenin' all,' he said, 'it's been a lovely day, has it not?' He spoke with the authority of a man who had seen it all. Blind since his sixth year, he could just remember the shapes and colours of the countryside. Those fragile memories were all he had to relieve his Guinness-black darkness. Still vivid was that last seeing moment. His sister on the swing, him pushing her away, mother calling 'Tea-time, children'. He had turned to say 'Coming Mum', meeting the full force of the oncoming swing at eye line.

O'Brien was rattling the bar with his empty glass.

'A drop of the real hard stuff now lad,' he instructed the spotty thin potboy. O'Brien was the head man round these parts. He ran the village grocery and took bets. He also had money in the bank, a cousin in America and a girl in the family way. Forty years old, though a little puffy in the face, he was still a handsome man. Like all men in Puckoon, he was married but single after six at night. When the war started he had, in a fit of drunken patriotism, joined the Connaught Rangers, gone to France, caught the crabs and won the v.c. Arriving home on leave, he was greeted like a hero, given a presentation casket of blue unction and then thrown into jail for having obscene French postcards in his haversack. Constable Millikudie had confiscated the offending pictures, and slaved all night duplicating another hundred. Disguised as a tout, he later sold them to visiting Americans. 'Genuine Dublin night life,' he told the startled tourists. As a result two American warships were crewless for a month while the sailors searched Dublin for the like.

O'Brien was joined by his friend, Dr Sean Goldstein. So Semitic did he look, that even at all-Hebrew parties people would say, 'Who's that Jewish-looking feller?' He had just come from the ailing Dan Doonan, where the patient had been complaining of a slight improvement.

'He's dying, for sure,' said Goldstein, parting a Guinness with his nose, 'It's a coronary condition. I give him the best drugs but, tsu, it's just a matter of time, which I suppose is the sentence we're all under.'

O'Brien lit a cigarette. 'I sometimes think,' he said, mixing his words with smoke, 'it would be kinder to do away with incurables.'

'Oh, nobody's incurable,' Goldstein was quick to reply. 'It's just that we don't know the cure, and remember, what's good for the dying is sometimes bad for the living.'

'Eh?'

'Well, if he dies I'm worse off. Work it out for yerself.'

'Oh, you're a hard man tell me, what's your feeling about abortions den?'

'You're a Catholic. You know the answer to that.'

'True, but what's your opinion as a medical man?'

'Murder.'

'How about that London surgeon? The girl had been raped and he took it away. Was he right or wrong?'

'I'll ask you the question which goes before that. Was the child right or wrong?'

O'Brien noticed a heated tone creeping into Goldstein's voice.

'Well Doc, at the time it wasn't *really* a child.'

'If it wasn't *really* a child O'Brien, what was all the fuss about?'

'Well,' began O'Brien, but was shut up by Goldstein –

'It's a bloody cosy little argument that, for the likes of get-rich-quick abortionists. It's not a child, it's just formed, it's just – it's just – just *anything* they want to call it to ease their bloody consciences! A mother sees her child born deformed due to some drug she took during pregnancy and has the child put to sleep! What *right* have we? When a man is mutilated in the war we don't kill him! *We* are the cowards. *We* can't stand seeing a deformed child. That child could grow up and enjoy life. Happiness is a state of mind, not body.

O'Brien paused, then drank his drink, thoughtfully.

'Oh yes, oh yes, I was in der fightin' all of der way.' Little Mister Pearce in the corner was holding forth. From a parchment dry face, locked under a flat cap, twinkling blue eyes peered through heavy pebble glass lenses, giving him the appearance of a goiterous elf. Both his weathered hands rested on a walking stick. 'In all the fightin' and the English never caught me.' He was speaking rapidly to a Mr Foggerty.

Foggerty wore a long, foul, ragged black overcoat, which seemed to have grown on him. It was secured round the middle with repeatedly knotted string, from which hung various accoutrements, mug, hair-brush, spoon, fly-swat, tin opener. An outsize greasy brown trilby, set low on his forehead, gave him the appearance of having no top to his head, which in fact he hadn't. Son of a long line of camp followers, he had been relieved of his post as lighthouse keeper at the shale rock when he drew the blinds, to 'stop the light shining into the poor sailors' eyes'. The light was closed down, and these days ships have to find their own way on to the rocks. His father had been drowned after a brawl on the edge of a whisky vat, not that he couldn't swim; he tried to drink his way out. Alcoholic poisoning was the Coroner's verdict.

'I tell you, he was so beautifully preserved, it seemed a shame ter bury him,' said the amazed mortician.

'Yes,' went on Mr Pearce, 'I was wounded twice, once by me own side.' He said it with the same surprise

as when it happened, and moved his biddy pipe to the other corner. 'You see, the Tans and the police was lookin' fer rebels; we was hid up in Clontarragh Street. One night we could hear them searchin' the places, all drunk. Finally they breaks into our place, they smashes up the furniture and lets fly a few rounds into the ceiling, me in the loft I gets it in the leg. In a few days it goes gangrene, so they smuggles in Goldstein and he offs with it. It was bloody murder, you should have seen the bill he sent me. Still, I survived.' He tapped his wooden leg with his pipe. 'It's hollow. . . . You know why?'

'No,' said Foggerty, nodding his head.

'It's hollow because I *made* it so. You see,' he puffed his pipe and looked up at the nicotined ceiling, 'Michael Leary wanted someone ter smuggle hand grenades out through the police cordon, so, I hollows me leg and I travels the bombs in that. And,' he laughed, 'they never caught me.'

Foggerty looked at Mr Pearce. Pearce looked at Mr Foggerty. It appeared to Foggerty that Mr Pearce had finished.

'Oh!' he said.

'Oh?' said Mr Pearce, 'Oh? I tell you a tale of Irish courage and hero-ism and all you can say is, Oh?'

Foggerty seemed to struggle with his mind. Gradually a pathetic smile spread over his face. 'Fish!' he said.

'Fish?' said Pearce, 'Fish? What about fish?'

'Well, it's different from "Oh".'

Mr Pearce just looked at Foggerty. There was

something amiss in this lad. Only that day someone had said 'Good morning' to him, and he seemed at a loss for a reply. Then again, Foggerty was the only one who had been a failure during the boom.

'You'da been in real trouble if dem bombs had gone off in yer leg, mate. Yer arse would ha' been half way up yer back.'

The voice came booming from Thomas Rafferty who stood six foot square. The pockets of his dark green jacket were congealed with blood, fur and feathers. When he wasn't poaching he was writing bits of poetry, but he lived by the trap. There was nothing like it. To sit on the banks of the Puckoon, eating a whole fresh salmon when the nobs in London were payin' ten shillings a slice for it. To walk on a silver cold moonlight night, in ankle-deep mist swirling in from the Atlantic; the repetitive crunch of boots on hard frost, hearing a barn owl shriek from the soot-black line of the venal trees, and the best of all the barking of a dog fox across the winter-tight countryside.

'Yarowwwww!' he gave an imitation. 'If that sound doesn't give you a thrill, youse dead,' he grinned, then upended a box of dominoes on the table.

'I'll give you a game,' said Foggerty, eagerly.

'No you bloody well don't!'

'I beat you last time.'

'I know you did and I haven't lived that down! Being beat by you is an admission of insanity, you stupid bloody idiot! No offence meant, mark you.'

Behind the bar, Mr O'Toole was speaking to the pig-of-a-face that was his wife. He had married her twenty years ago, but still woke up white and sweating. On leave from France, he had come out of a drinking-hole in Sackville Street and bumped into a girl. It was dark, he was drunk, she was keen. He awoke next morning to find her in bed with him. He ran screaming from the house, her purse under his arm. He didn't get away with it. Seven weeks later, a giant of a man, seven foot high and smothered in red hair, walked through the door holding her by the hand. The monster lifted O'Toole off the floor and told him to get ready 'for marriage or death'. He had started to object, where-upon the monster had started to hit him with great bone-crunching knuckles. All he remembered was birds twittering and her shouting 'Don't ruin him for the honeymoon, hit him above the waist.' Leaving a trail of broken teeth he was dragged to the altar in the grip of two monsters who looked like kinfolk of Grendel.

Finally, when the priest asked 'Will you take this woman – ' a hired ventriloquist from Cork said, 'I do.' And he was done. The marriage hadn't turned out too bad, well, actually it had, but otherwise it wasn't too bad. The red monster, her father, had died mysteriously of heart failure after falling under a train but not before willing them the Holy Drinker.

'Where's the Milligan tonight, Maudie?'

'I don't know. He was here this morning trying to cadge a drink,' she replied, looking over his shoulder at the handsome O'Brien. She had, in moments of dreaming eroticism, imagined herself clutching his members under the sheets. Whenever she saw a sign 'Members Only' she thought of him. The pub door opened, and in bore a podgy police uniform carrying the body of Sgt MacGillikudie. There was a rush for the door. He held up a calming hand but was knocked flat by the exodus.

Arising, he dusted himself.

'I'll be glad when dis town gets prison cells with locks on. Now – ' he felt in his breast pocket, '– I'm here to read a brief notice.' He removed his helmet and inadvertently placed it over Blind Devine's beer. 'To all Citizens of the Free State,' he commenced.

His speech was hesitant and clipped; a black Lord Kitchener moustache cut his face in two. 'Next week military and civil members of the Ulster Boundary Commission will be passing through this area. Any hostility towards them will be penalized with fines from a shilling up to death. Ah, tank you – ' he accepted a free beer from O'Toole. 'Cheers!' he said and drained it to eternity. Blind Devine was groping.

'Some thievin' swine's stolen me beer!' he shouted angrily as only the blind have courage to.

'You might ha' drunk it.'

'I never forget any beer I drink!' shouted Devine. He flourished his stick, striking Foggerty a sickening blow on the shin.

'Owwww!' screamed Foggerty, clutching his elbow.

'Here, man,' said O'Toole, giving Devine a beer, 'drink this on the house and calm down.'

'Well, I'll be on me way now,' said MacGillikudie, picking up his helmet.

'What's this, then?' said O'Toole, pointing to the glass of beer revealed.

39

'Oh, dat's mine,' said Foggerty, who was not such a fool after all.

'Come on, Stan lad,' said O'Brien, 'give us one of yer love songs, one of dem with all the strains.'

The spotty lad gave Mrs O'Toole an appealing look.

'All right then, we're not too busy.'

Despite the absence of a piano player, the lad came and stood dutifully by the mute instrument.

'Ladies and Gentlemen – ' he began.

'Order, please.'

'Silence for the singer.'

'Is it free?'

The lad went on: 'I should like to sing the late J. Collard Jackson's lovely song "*Eileen, My Eileen*."'

He raised the lid of the beer-saturated piano, struck a note and started singing a different one. The lad opened a raw red mouth, revealing great harp strings of saliva. At first no sound same, then, welling from the back of his body there came a quivering, tense, tinny sound, like a tram issuing from a tunnel. With the arrival of the first uncertain note, the lad's eyes glazed over, as though a stricture of the bowels was imminent; the singer's body went rigid, a series of stomach convulsions ensued, then the whole body quivered. It even frightened Dr Goldstein.

> 'Eileeeeeeeeeeeeeen!
> Yoooou arrree my Queeeeennnn . . .'

The agonized notes seemed to swell up from the thorax and pass hurriedly inwards towards the back of the head, where they were apparently trapped and reduced by a three-inch cavity skull; rebounding, they escaped by struggling down one side of his clogged nose at strength three.

> 'My Queeeeeeeeeeeeenn
> The finest I've ever seeeeeeeeeeeeeen . . .'

Puzzled spectators observed that his lower jaw, unlike yours or mine, remained static; it was the *top* of his head that moved. On high notes it was so acutely angled, most of the time was spent looking up the singer's nose, a terrible sight to behold. He indulged in an orgy of meaningless gestures, even the word 'it' was sung, trembling with catarrhal extasy; time and again he raised his skinny arms to heaven, revealing a ragged armpit from which protruded tufts of brown hair. Veins stood out on his forehead, and sweat ran down his face as, purple with strain, he braced himself for the last great note; bending his knees, clenching his fists, he closed his eyes and threw back his head. In that tacit moment the observant Foggerty spoke:

'Hey, Mister, you got a bogey up yer nose.'

The last great note burst and was lost in a sea of irreverent laughter. Red-faced, tears drowning his eyes, he returned to the bar. The world of music was safer by far and J. Collard Jackson stopped turning in his grave.

The air outside was still and humid. Without warning, the sky lit up in a moment of fluorescent anger: a fistful of thunder racketed over Puckoon. 'God save us all from the Protestant thunder,' gasped two wax-white old biddies, clutching their bedclothes and making arthritic signs of the cross. 'Quick, Millie, the Po,' gasped the elder sister.

'Coming, coming, Sarah!'

'Too late, Millie, too late.' The reply came in a long, damp moan.

Cool spindles of long-fingered rain came racing to the eager ground. Earth gurgled under the delicious assault, the attarahent smell of earth and water wedded came wafting from the ground. Heavier and heavier it fell. Even at this late hour, ducks on the village pond could be heard acclaiming the deluge. The whole sky was a cullender of water. Again and again lightning hurried across the sky, blossoming like electric roses; the temperature fell, the closeness split, a great song of silence followed.

Millie was changing the bed linen, spiders tested their webs and a drunk called Hermonogies K. Thuckrutes lay face down in a gutter, singing softly.

'Good, we could have done with that little lot,' said O'Brien, looking out the pub window.

Outside there was a strange muffled sound. The pub door opened slowly, and there, reeling, smoke-blackened, and smelling strangely of burnt rubber and singed flesh, was the near-carbonized figure of the Milligan. The whole pub turned inwards as he entered. Someone made the sign of the cross.

'Is it the devil?' said Blind Devine, hiding his matches. Milligan took his still smouldering cap and hurled it the length of the room.

42

'Struck by lightning! That's all I needed was to be struck by bloody lightning!'

'Are you all right?' asked Dr Goldstein, handing him his professional card.

'It was only the rubber tyres on me bike saved me from being electrified. It struck the roots of a tree, bounced on ter me legs then travelled up to me head! Me hat, look at me hat!' he said, picking up the charred relic.

'Here,' said Mrs O'Toole, 'drink this.' She handed him a small measure of cheap whisky. Even in moments of charity there was no need to be uneconomical.

Through all this commotion, through all the thunder, singing and drinking, from the opposite wall two humans stared unwinking at each other, eyes choked with mutual hate, fury and frustration.

She was Mrs Cafferty, he was known to her as Mr Cafferty, and there's no divorce in Ireland. But enough of this. Elsewhere important things were happening.

Chapter Four

It was to be a solemn occasion. As James Joyce says, 'real hairy'. In a brown and upstairs room at the Duke of Wellington Hotel 'Ireland', to quote an I.R.A. leaflet, was being 'torn in two by TRATERS', the last word being in red. At every door and window, standing, sitting, looking, listening, soldiers from both factions stood guard. Beyond them, another perimeter of men set off as listening posts. With the I.R.A. about, nobody was taking any chances, least of all the I.R.A. who were all home in bed. Rain was falling, and the men stood close to the walls for shelter. Inside, several high-ranking, grim-faced Boundary Commissioners from both sides faced each other across a giant map of Ireland.

On one corner rested a mess of empty tea cups; half-eaten sandwiches, their edges curling, lay helpless in a thin film of tea that trembled on the floor of the tray. Lighting the scene was a mean yellow bulb covered with generations of fly specks. Across the map, running from right to left, was a thick red pencil line that terminated just short of the Atlantic. It was the threatened new border. In its path lay sleeping Puckoon. Points of interest and under discussion were represented by a forest of little flags on pins, forever being displaced by table-thumping members of the Commission. For ten whole days now they had argued the last few miles of frontier. Tempers were frayed, agreements infrequent and weak bladders put to the test. Mr Haggerty was complaining about the Ulster representatives' indecisiveness.

He was breathing heavily from a short fat round body packed into a blue serge suit, every seam of which was under considerable pressure from the contents. He lost his temper and – more frequently – his arguments.

'You'll *all* be in the Republic one day, so there,' he thumped the map with a fat furious fist, displacing numerous flags.

Immediately, Mr Neville Thwick, a thin, veiny, eel-like man with acne, deftly replaced the flags. He had volunteered for the job. Insignificant since birth, sticking pins in maps gave him the secret power he craved. The walls of his attic bed-sitting room were hung with treasured maps of famous battles, campaigns and sorties. Solfarino, Malplaquet, Plassey, the Somme, the Boyne. There were three hundred in scrolls under his bed and scores more, carefully indexed, placed on every shelf and ledge. He possessed his own pin-making machine, and a small triangular printers' guillotine for manufacturing flags. Power, what power this combination held!

Every night Mr Thwick would leave his desk at Mills & Crotts bird-seed factory and catch the 33a tram to his home. On arrival he would prepare tea and perhaps a one-egg omelette. After a wash and shave he would place a battle-map of his choosing on the floor. From a chest he would select a military uniform suitable for the period. Dressed so, he would pace the room, making little battle noises with his mouth. Last Sunday had seen his greatest victory. After much deliberation he had decided to re-contest Waterloo. Dressed as Napoleon he placed himself at the head of the French army of 600 flags. The thought of it had made him weak, he felt giddy and sat down to massage his legs. After a measure of ginger wine, he felt strong enough to continue. There followed a night of move and counter move. Despite knockings on the walls from sleepless neighbours, he continued his battle noises, thrusting flags hither and thither. He force-marched a platoon of French Chasseurs till their points were blunt, he reinforced Blucher with a secret supply of mercenary flags from Ireland and destroyed the Prussian threat to his flank. At three o'clock he played his master stroke. He thrust a white flag right into the English H.Q.

Wellington and his staff were humbled in the dust. To the accompaniment of the people around hammering with shoe heels and brooms, he accepted Wellington's sword and surrender. Then victorious to bed with a hot water bottle and a spoonful of Dr Clarkson-Spock's Chest Elixir. Next morning, dressed as a civilian, with very little resistance, Wellington's conqueror was evicted by his landlady.

Living in the Y.M.C.A. curtailed his activities, but the present job kept him in practice until conditions changed. After all, peace, as any good general knew, couldn't last for ever, and the only way to *end* wars was to have them.

'Mr Haggerty, sir.' The febrile, castrato voice of Mr Meredith was raised in protest. 'Mr Haggerty,' he repeated, as he rose to his feet. One could see how very old he was, how very thin he was, and falling back into his seat, how very weak he was. 'Mr Haggerty,' he said for the third time, his pale hands flapping like mating butterflies, 'I protest at –'. He stopped suddenly, eyes closed, lids quivering, head back. 'Ahhhhhh – AHHHHH – ' A pause, his face taking on that agonized look of the unborn sneeze. 'Sorry about that,' he muttered, wiping his eyes. 'Now.' He became stronger. 'I was saying th – ATISHOOOOO!' thundered the unexpected; 'AH-TISHOOOO!!' The convulsion shot his dentures the length of the room. Thud! went his head on the table, 'ATISHOO!' *down* went the flags, *in* sprang Mr Thwick. 'Oh!' shrieked Mrs Eels, a set of heavy dentures landing on her lap. Meredith lay back, spit-speckled, white and exhausted, his face folded in two.

Mrs Eels returned his teeth on a plate covered with her 'kerchief. 'No thank you, dear,' said the still muzzy Meredith, 'I couldn't eat another thing.'

With his back to the map table and accompanied by terrifying clicks and clacks, Meredith wrestled to replace his prodigal dentures; finally, he turned to continue his speech, but remained silent. Staring pop-eyed, he staggered round the room pointing to his mouth, making mute sounds and getting redder and redder.

'Ahhhh! I see what the trouble is,' said Haggerty, pulling down Meredith's lower lip. 'He's put his choppers in upside down, someone fetch me a screw-driver.'

Mr Meredith's aide-de-camp, Captain Clarke,

called for a short pause while 'our spokesman's dentures are readjusted and his dignity restored'. A regular soldier, he was known to his subordinates as 'Here comes the bastard now'. The phrenology of his mountainous skull showed in contours through his military hair-cut. Erect and shining, his immaculate uniform hid a mess of ragged underwear.

'No, no, no,' said Mrs Angel Eels, 'we've had enough delays, we got to finish this partitioning – today!'

There was a murmur of approval. She glowed inwardly at their acceptance. She was a true daughter of the revolution, a tireless worker for the Party, sexually frustrated and slightly cross-eyed, the last two having something in common. At forty-one years of age, she now sat bolt upright, her black dress fastened high under her neck down to the floor, worn like a chastity armour that sealed her from all harm, and pleasure.

Her late husband, Frederick Mortimer Eels, had been a professional circus midget. Twice nightly he was fired from a cannon into a net. That and cleaning out the elephants was his job, though he only got billed for the former. Angel had met him by accident. She ran over him in her gig. Born with an abnormal fear of men, Angel saw in Frederick all the innocence of boyhood. Lying in hospital under drugs from the accident, Frederick had proposed to her.

Courting her in public was difficult, as she towered over him by three feet, and he made a point of only meeting her on the side of a hill. As the wedding day approached Fred Eels was seized with a sexual phobia.

'Ha, ha, ha,' said the doctor, 'there's no need to worry, Fred. I've known far shorter men marry far taller women and they've had a perfectly normal sex life. Of course,' he added, 'you won't have anybody to talk to.'

Love does something. At the wedding, Angel, for all her plainness, looked beautiful, and even Mr Eels looked and walked a foot taller. It was not to last. The honeymoon was fatal. Trying to change a light bulb in the bridal suite, Fred balanced on a chair and table, fell back in the dark, broke his neck, and died. The funeral, tho' purple sad, seemed a grim joke. The child-sized coffin lowered into the man-sized grave.

'I'm sorry, Father,' an embarrassed grave-digger apologized, 'I thought it was her husband.'

'It is,' whispered the priest.

'They must have buried him doubled up,' the digger told his wife that night. 'Some people will do anything to save money.'

Since then, fifteen long years ago, Mrs Eels had no other love, but she had visited many, many circuses. In that time, frustration had snowballed and was thundering down the slopes of desire. It was a strange thing to be a widow and a virgin; secretly there were times she would have loved to have run naked down O'Connell Street, shouting 'I've just slept with a nigger man and this is me lunch break.' All this was now sublimated in the false zeal of a female patriot.

By levering hard with the screwdriver and smashing four teeth, Haggerty had managed to release Meredith's dentures.

Till now, monkey-faced Mr Ferguson had said little; now, drawing a breath he spoke in a sing-song manner.

'May I make a suggestion? We only have this bit here to partition and the pubs close in an hour. Why not let's all put one hand on the red pencil and draw a line that falls naturally and peacefully into place?'

As he spoke his nose twitched, violently, an affliction from the Boer War. His regiment had camped near Spion Cop; the area was strewn with spherical white rocks like tennis balls. Issuing from his tent one morning, he saw three soldiers throwing a rock around.

'Over here,' shouted the enthusiastic soccer player.

It sailed towards him, he removed his hat, jumped, headed it and fell smiling and unconscious.

That's when it started. Mr Ferguson didn't mind. It got him out of the fighting with a disability pension. Twice annually he would report to a medical board who decided whether the affliction was diminishing. The day before these occasions, he would soak his nose in arnica and pull a tight elastic band over his head and down under his nose, thus holding it in a contracted position all night. The moment before the medical, he would remove the band, and the nose, sensing its freedom, shook with terrifying flexibility. So well had it behaved last time, the Board had increased his pension by a half.

But back to now. On a show of hands, they accepted his suggestion. In what was meant to be a solemn moment, all hands held the pencil and pulled slowly across the map. All was silent, the room was filled with suspicion. Occasionally a gasp rent the silence as they all strained for the advantage.

'Steady, someone's pulling to the benefit of Ulster.'

'Lies, all lies.'

'Who gave that jerk?'

'Ah! I felt that.'

'Swine!'

Finally the pencil reached its destination. Faces broke into relieved smiles, and a series of rapid unplanned handshakes ensued.

'His hands feel nice,' thought Angel.

Haggerty rang a bell. A Free State soldier entered the room.

'Pardon me, sir,' he said respectfully, his face lost in the obscurity of an overlarge cap, 'there are two men outside says they're the photographers.'

'Send them in,' said the gleeful Haggerty.

The soldier saluted, and turned smartly about face, still leaving his cap facing forwards.

Two morturial men entered the room. One was taller than the other as is often the case in Ireland. Dressed in black and wearing top hats they carried a coffin-like box into the room. The small one proffered a card.

Cole Brothers
Professional Morticians
Amature Photographers

The tall one possessed long bony fingers that crackled and snapped with healthy young rheumatism.

'I'll scream if he touches me,' thought Angel.

The tall one appeared to be in charge, that is, he did less work than the other, which is usually a sign of authority. He made the short brother do his bidding with sibilant whispers and frequent nips on the buttocks. The little Cole brother worked under two difficulties – a stiff collar that lodged high under his throat and a new truss that played merry hell with his testicles.

With polite interest and light conversation they all watched as the Brothers Cole assembled a scaffold of legs and equipment. Captain Clarke took to circling the apparatus, pausing now and then to tap the tripod authoritatively with his regimental cane.

'Good,' he would say crisply, 'very good.' He tapped once more and the structure collapsed.

'If you'd try not doin' that, it would help,' said the little Cole. Finally, 'If the fine ladies and gentlemen will take up thoughtful poses, we will record the occasion.'

The tall Cole beckoned Mrs Eels with a crackling finger. 'If the lady will please be seated.'

'Just a minute,' interrupted white-haired Mr Brogan, who had said nothing for three days but been under suspicion for stomach offences, 'no ill-will, mark you, but me being the oldest member here, I think *I* should be the central figure, me and me fine white head of hair.'

He was ignored to a man, him, *and* his fine white head of hair. There were problems. Mrs Eels' cross eyes.

'If madam would sit profile,' was the respectful

suggestion. Meredith smiled blissfully, forgetful of his missing teeth. Behind Mr Thwick, a hatstand grew from his head; the ears of Capt. Clarke, sitting cross-legged on the floor, stood out in terrifying relief against Angel's black dress, like the handles of the F.A. Cup.

'Keep your nose still, Mr Ferguson!'

'Sorry, lad, it only stops if I stick me finger up it.'

'Do that then, or it'll come out blurred.'

Ferguson dutifully thrust his finger into position, his bow legs framing the fireplace behind, the flames disappearing up his seat. Stretched majestically across the front, head in hand, was handsome Councillor Andrew Burke, looking stern and intelligent, unaware that he had recently forgotten to adjust his dress before leaving. 'I wonder where that draught's coming from,' he thought. Mr Brogan, still in a huff, stood with his back to the camera. 'I might as well show me fine white head of hair,' he thought. The magnesium flared, everybody blinked. It was over.

Mrs Eels married the taller Cole Brother. Apparently, when posing her, his hand had touched her knee. He survived the honeymoon, which was ruined for her, the hotel manager had been a midget.

Chapter Five

Belfast is a big city. At one time it was quite small, even worse, there has been an occasion when there was no Belfast City at all. Thank heaven, those days are gone and there is now a plentiful supply of Belfast. Ugly and grey it spreads out, drab, dull, lack-lustre streets, crammed with the same repetitive, faceless, uninspired, profit-taking, soul-breaking buildings. The only edifices worth seeing are those erected long before the coming of the local council and the builder. Beautiful buildings seemed to taunt them. 'Pull them down!' was the cry. 'The Highway must go through.' The world, beauty, tranquillity and fresh air were being sacrificed to a lump of compressed tin with a combustion engine. Stately trees were felled as a 'Danger to lightning', and when one questioned them the answer came from a faceless thing called 'Spokesman said'. Here, safe in its bureaucratic cocoon, we had the new vandalism of authority, power without conscience or taste; as it was with Belfast so was it with other cities, for now and ever after it seemed. In this metropolis lived many citizens. Most of them poor, with an additional burden, nowadays it costs more to be poor than it used to.

Inside sternly furnished wallpapered rooms at number 356 Queen Victoria Crescent, two young Customs officers were packing well-travelled suitcases.

Webster was short and handsomish, with ill-cut

straight brown hair and grey eyes, all in all a bit of a ladies' man, one bit in particular. By comparison, Peter Barrington, his tall, blond, rather wavering room-mate, looked slightly effeminate. The two had nothing in common save the English language, and even then Barrington had a superior accent for it. As they packed, the tops of the red buses passed and repassed the windows with their never ending pageant of adverts. 'Beechams worth a guinea a box', 'Take Andrews Little Liver . . .' 'Gynon Salts for the regular. . . .' 'Exlax'.

The motive seemed to be 'Make people shit and get rich'. Strange, people won't believe in God, yet will swear by some blue pill that guarantees to rid them of baldness, bedwetting, distended kidneys, pox and varicose veins. Piles! A man with piles will believe any promise of a cure. Sitting on clusters of sore and distended veins, his mind goes awry and his judgement uncertain. Judge Jeffreys suffered from piles, and look at the havoc he wrought on the unfortunate followers of Monmouth. If it hadn't been for piles, Monmouth would have been alive today! Unaware of this historical truth, Barrington and Webster packed their cases.

'I cwan't sae I fwancy lwiving under cwanvas,' said Barrington, his accent almost obliterating the meaning of the words.

The upper class sound of it ruffled Webster. He didn't like Barrington, but two sharing a room was cheaper than one. Webster's background was Poplar, docks, dirt, pubs. He had been born in a cockney family when cockneys were perfectly content with

55

their lot, made good workmen, great craftsmen, superb soldiers and were the first to put up flags for the King and Queen. In the twenty-five years since World War I that had all changed; gradually the adulation for the Crown grew less and less. Queen Victoria had gone to her grave with the streets choked with mourning citizens; it was a very thin funeral crowd that watched King George VI to his rest; it followed that the funeral of our present Queen was going to be downright embarrassing.

Behind the throne desperate efforts were made by those whose jobs hang by royal decree, to modify the Royal Family to meet the Social Revolution and make their little jobs more secure. The speech-writer royal was also under fire from the press; he had used the 'My husband and I' opening so frequently that it was always good for a laugh in comedy shows, and B.B.C. variety departments chiefs in search of O.B.E.s were quick to strike it from scripts, one of their rare positive gestures.

Barrington lit a cigarette. Unlike Webster, Barrington had been born into a class that denied him the joy of self-accomplishment; it had been all 'laid in' for him. His name was down for Eton three years before his birth, gilt-edged godparents, his baptism could be seen in *The Tatler*, *London Illustrated* and, in *The Times* a small notice to that effect. Despite all this he had been cashiered from the Guards for a certain incident with a young boy. It had been given three-inch headlines in all Sunday papers, those Sunday papers that are always both 'shocked and distressed' at crime and degradation; so shocked and distressed are they, that every Sunday they re-shock themselves as a 'Public Duty'. THIS MUST BE STOPPED! says the front page.

Then the copy: Police Raid Den of Vice! Sixteen-year-old white girl found with black men! Working on information from one of our reporters, Scotland Yard Vice Squads this morning raided a Greek Club in Soho. Sgt. Henshaw C.I.D. reported seeing a hundred and twenty couples playing Bingo in the nude; when questioned the proprietor, Knessis Philominides, said that the players had felt 'hot'. Police removed certain appliances, an eight millimetre film projector, along with some films. Names and addresses were taken, among them eighteen-year-old the Hon. Maureen Campbell-Torrington of Bayswater. She was escorted by Pandit Nowarajee Gupta, Hindu seaman of no fixed abode. He told a Paddington magistrate, 'I had two whiskies and a small port wine and everything went black. When I regained my sensibilities I was in a Black Maria handcuffed to ten other men who were also naked.' Asked to explain 40 lbs of heroin in his pugaree he said, 'You are only doing this because you think I am Jewish!' He then showed them a photo of Ghandi and claimed diplomatic immunity.

In the same way, poor Barrington had been exposed to the nation.

His mother, Lady Norah, had been singularly unmoved by it all. As she told a reporter, 'I can't understand all the fuss, his father did this sort of thing all the time, and he got on *awfully* well,' but then she added, 'He worked in the Foreign Office.' An educated woman, she spoke eight languages and said nothing intelligent in any of them. She was one of those pale, powder-white, sedentary creatures who no matter when you called was always cutting flowers in the garden. As wars broke out she couldn't wait to start rolling bandages and knitting things for those 'poor men at the front'; in peacetime she ignored them completely. Lord Barrington himself was a devout Catholic and a practising homosexual; as he frequently said, 'practice makes perfect'. He was a fine military figure, and why shouldn't he be. From his ankles to his groins he wore Dr Murray's anti-varicose elastic stockings; from groins to mid-rib he wore severe male corsets, made secretly by Marie Lloyd's dresser; around his shoulders, laced under his armpits and knotted at the back were 'Clarke's elastic posture braces'; his glass eye gazed unseeing at the world, into its live companion was screwed a monocle. A stickler for fitness, he spent every morning lying on the floor clenching and unclenching his fists. In the 14–18 affair, he served as one of Haig's military asses, saluting, pointing at maps, walking behind V.I.P.s, shaking hands, posing for photographs and forever reminding the General his fly buttons were in full view of enemy snipers, and so won Haig's undying gratitude. Now his young son Hon. Barrington had been seconded to the temporary obscurity of the Northern Irish Customs. Webster and he were both due to organize a Customs Post along the new border near Puckoon.

'Where the hell *is* Puckoon?' Webster was about to ask, when there was a combined knocking and opening of the door, the speciality of landladies in need of scandal, as was Mrs Cafferty: standing there, her bones almost escaping from her body, she smiled a great mouthful of rotten teeth, a salute to poverty and indifferent dentistry.

'I'm sorry yer goin' at such short notice,' she grinned, and handed the bill to Barrington.

'Two pounds?'

'That's one pound in lieu of a week's notice, sir.'

Barrington placed his cigarette on the window sill and took a five pound note from a registered envelope. From 'Mummy'.

'Oh,' said Mrs Cafferty, 'I'm sorry, we don't take cheques, sir.'

'Cheques? This is a five pound note.'

Confused and baffled by her ignorance of the higher currency denominations, she backed from the room, clutching the front of her flowered apron.

'I'll bring me husband up, he knows all about dem tings.'

Downstairs, his socks singeing in the heat of a near red stove, dozed the lord and master of the house. Robert Cafferty. Deep down in a fast disintegrating imitation leather armchair, he smouldered in mid-evening sleep. Around him his kingdom. On the stove, a blue chipped teapot was stewing the last life from its imprisoned leaves; on the mantelpiece a clockwork Virgin Mary, made in Japan.

'Wake up, darlin',' said Mrs Cafferty, striking him gently with her clenched fist.

'Ouch!' yelled Cafferty, leaping to his socks. 'Wassermarre, I'll kill the son of a –'

'Look at this,' she waved the five pound note.

'Oh,' he donned his glasses. 'It's a cheque . . . isn't it?'

'That's what I told dem, but dem says no.'

'I'll talk to dems.' He pulled up his braces and put his hat on as a sign of authority.

Webster and Barrington could hear them coming up the stairs in a flurry of whispers.

'Good morning to you both,' said Cafferty, appearing in the doorway, his face still drugged with sleep. 'Well, well – ' he looked round the room in mock surprise, 'so you're leaving,' and without a break, 'Sorry we don't take cheques.'

Barrington snatched the note from Cafferty's hand, tearing it in half. 'For God's sake,' he said angrily, snatching the remaining half, leaving behind yet a smaller piece.

The Caffertys moved together for safety.

'Here!' Barrington hastily counted out four brown ten shilling notes. 'Brown, *dat's* the colour of money,' thought Cafferty.

'Sorry, we don't take dem cheques,' he said, leaving the room.

They could hear her hitting Cafferty as he stumbled down the stairs. One hour later Webster and Barrington sat side by side on hard black leather seats rocking sleepily on the train to Puckoon. Back in 356 Queen Victoria Road, Barrington's cigarette on the window sill was burning the house down.

'Hello, Hello, Prudential?' said the smoke enveloped Cafferty, 'Hello? I want to take out a fire policy . . .'

A most irreverent wind whistled through the seams of Major Stokes' military trousers. The rain whip-lashed his violent overcast face. In the damp shadows behind stood members of his platoon, their identity lost in the timeless obscurity of a railway waiting room. There was no light, and the building was dank. The roof leaked, the gutters leaked, his hat leaked. He took a pull on his brandy flask.

'Puckoon! What a God-forsaken place.' He paced the weed-soaked platform breathing minced oaths. He stopped and beat a rapid military tattoo on his riding boot. 'Ouch!' he said. Stepping crisply into the street lamp's crepuscular glow, he took a nickel military watch from his pocket. The military time was nineteen hundred hours. The train was late. He rapped loudly on the ticket office partition; from behind came the sound of a rusty bolt being withdrawn; the partition slid half-way up, jammed, then slammed down again; a second time it rose, this time framed in the Gothic aperture was the unshaven, sandwich-chewing face of the Station Master, Donald Feeley. He peered into the dark at the Major's wet, white face.

'Where are you goin' to, sorr?'

'I'm not going anywhere.'

'Good, then you've arrived. Good night.'

'Wait,' the Major restrained him. 'I'm waiting for the train that was due here at sixteen hundred, the time is now nineteen hundred hours, you know what that means?'

'Nineteen hundred hours? No, sorr, my watch only goes up to twelve.'

'It's *three hours late* man! I'm supposed to pick up two Customs officers.'

'Oh?'

'Can't you 'phone, or something?'

'Dere's no 'phone here. We got a letter box.'

He stuffed another sandwich in his mouth.

'Is it usually this late?' shouted the Major, becoming openly vituperative.

'I meself have never timed it. Long as it goes backwards and forwards that's all we care.' He coughed, showering the Major with pointillisms of bread and sardines.

'You're a blasted idiot!' said the Major.

'True, sir, very true,' said Feeley, closing the partition.

Turning away in a fury, the Major fell heavily over a box. The darkness was filled with clucking chickens and swearing. 'What bloody idiot left that crate there?'

'I did,' said a voice.

He struck a match. It was a nun. This was all getting intolerable. He thought of London and Penelope, he thought of London and his wife, finally he thought of London and himself. A proud man.

A blow to Major Clarke's vanity had been going bald at the tender age of twenty-six while serving in Southern Command India. He had tried a remedy suggested by a doctor, Chanditje Lalkaka. Wagging his head, in a Welsh chee-chee accent, the Hindu physician had explained, 'It is made from a secret Punjabi formula, captured by Shivaji from the Rajputs during the Marhatta wars.' A bald man is a desperate man; but a bald *vain* man is a hairless Greek Tragedy.

The Major paid Lalkaka one hundred rupees. For five days and nights he sat in a darkened room, his head covered in a mixture of saffron cowdung and a curry-soaked handkerchief. Issuing forth on the sixth day, he discovered that what little hair he had had disappeared and so had Dr Lalkaka. For years after that he habitually and suddenly hit unsuspecting passing wogs and pointed to his head. Meanwhile, he took another pull at his flask and peered up the track into the sightless night.

Four miles up the line, showing no signs of life, was the six-thirty train for Puckoon. The carriage lights, strung like amber beads, hung lustreless in the squalling rain. A weak trickle of steam hissed from the outlet valve. On the foot-plate, O'Malley, the ginger-haired fireman, looked at the dead furnace.

'I can't understand it! Dat coal bunker was full on Thursday.'

'Well, it's *Friday* and *empty*,' said Driver Murtagh.

'Don't lose yer temper, Murtagh, all we need is somethin' to burn.'

'Oh! Wid a fine mind like that you're wasting yer time as fireman, and you're also wastin' *mine*!' Murtagh drummed his fingers in the throttle and spat into the dark.

'Now den! you listen to *me*! We passed a cottage a few yards back. Go and see if they've got a couple of buckets o' coal or peat.'

'O.K.' said O'Malley, and he climbed down and

crunched off into the darkness. From the carriages came enquiries.

'What we stopped for, mister?'

'Is this Dublin?'

'What happens if we can't get started?'

'Well,' explained O'Malley, 'First class passengers will be taken on by private car.'

'What about us third class?'

'You get out and bloody well push.'

He continued on past the carriages, ignoring several cat-calls, two empty bottles and a passenger who couldn't hold it any longer. The cottage was dark save for a light in the back. There was no knocker. Hands in pockets, he tapped with his foot.

'Who's there?' said a female voice.

'Please, mam', it's the fireman from the Puckoon Flyer.'

'Did you fall off, then?'

'No, we've runned out of fuel.'

The door opened, a girl's face appeared, it appeared very pretty too.

'Come in.'

'Oh, tanks.'

The room was plain, a fire burned in a large inglenook recess. A crucifix and holy pictures hung on the far wall – a red light burned at a small altar. 'What is it you want?'

'Could we borrow a couple of buckets of coal or peat?'

'Coal I have. Would you like a cup of tea before you go? You look awful wet.'

He shuffled his feet.

'Aw, come on,' she said, pushing him back into a chair. 'That train's never been on time.'

She kept looking at him in a way. He sipped his cup of tea. She was looking at him in that way again . . . he finished his cup of tea. . . .

Dear reader, it's a wonder how one bed can take so much punishment. The springs groaned under the combined assault of two activated bodies. It was an age-old story but neither of them seemed to have heard it before, and, they did it *all* on *one* cup of tea. Dear friends, a quarter of a pound of tea can be bought for as little as two shillings, and think of the fun you can have in the privacy of your own home.

From outside came an angry knocking on the door, from inside came an agonized coitus interruptus. 'Oh God,' gasped O'Malley, rolling off, 'who can it be?'

'How the hell do I know?' She was pulling on skirt, petticoat, stockings, but no drawers – after all this could be a false alarm. O'Malley wrestled frantically to tuck an unruly member into his trousers.

'Anybody in?' came the voice.

Relief showed on O'Malley's face. 'It's all right, it's me mate.'

The door opened on a wet engine driver. 'What the blazes has – ' He saw the girl. 'Oh,' he said.

Carrying the buckets of coal back up the line O'Malley confided, 'Hey, you know why I was so long?'

'Sure,' grinned the driver, 'I was watching through the window. My, you've got a spotty bum.'

Saturday. Pay day! Ha, ha, Milligan rubbed his

hands. Six days grass cutting at three shillings a day, six multiplied by three – 12 shillings! Ha! Ha! He looked at the church clock. 4.32. Time for lunch! He unwrapped brown bread, cheese, boiled potatoes and a bottle of stout. He took a long drink on the bottle and a long eat on the bread. By Gor, the old woman was starting to look after him dese days, perhaps work was the answer after all. The sun was warm again, he stretched out on a gently sloping gravestone. A breeze turned the trees into a rataplan of skirling leaves. He watched a cluster waving overhead. I wonder if they enjoy doing that? It looks as if they are. He finished his meal. Four thirty two! Just enough time for an hour's forty winks.

Milligan was awakened by the approach of an internal combustion engine. He could see the occupants. Polis! *And* the military! He dived instinctively into a pile of cut grass. There was a tread of military boots up the drive. They stopped.

'Anybody about?'

An English voice! What the hell were they doin' back here?

'Hello,' came the voice again. Through the lattice of grass, he could see a Corporal. He heard a soft gurgle as the soldier drained the last of his stout. 'I'll get him for that,' swore Milligan. A second man approached. It was Major Stokes. Milligan didn't know it was Major Stokes, but that doesn't alter the fact that that is who it was. They were joined by Sgt. MacGillikudie.

'Any signs of life, Corporal?' A strange question in a graveyard.

'No sir. There must be somebody around, I just found this empty Guinness bottle.'

'Can I help you, gentlemen?' The voice of Father Rudden came on the scene.

'Ah, Vicar,' said Major Stokes. *Vicar?* The priest shuddered.

'My name's Stokes, o.c. 2/4 Ulster Rifles.' He extended his hand, had it crushed and returned.

'And what can we do for you, *Mister* Stokes?'

'We're here to build the new Customs Post and erect border fences.'

'Er – I don't see how I can help, I've got a bad back.'

The Major didn't seem to hear, he produced an Ordnance Survey map and pointed to a small red circle. 'This here is where it's to be, which lies approximately – ' he pointed – 'over there.' The priest raised his eyebrows. 'A Customs shed? On CHURCH ground? I've heard nothing of this, it must be a mistake.'

'No, it's true, Father,' interrupted MacGillikudie, 'I had this official letter this morning.' Rudden glanced through it quickly. 'Well,' he concluded, 'I've received no notification, I shall have to write to Cardinal MacQueen in Dublin about it.'

'Can't wait for that, Vicar,' said Stokes. 'We have instructions to start right away.' Rudden rubbed his chin. 'Very well, if it's the law I can't stop it, but I think it's damnable to run a frontier through a church-yard.' He stormed back to the church ignoring the Major's attempts to explain. 'He'll be all right, sir,' said MacGillikudie with assurance. 'He's a fine man, he'll always give you a hand.'

'It'll be a long time before I give him mine again,' said the Major, feeling for broken bones.

Dan Milligan in his grass prison, realized now there was no cause for alarm. He sprang to his feet like a herbal phantom. 'Good morning all,' he said happily.

'It's someone risen from the dead,' said the terrified MacGillikudie.

'Hands up,' said the startled Major.

'Don't shoot,' said the grassy spectre. 'it's *me*, Dan Milligan, aged 41.'

The Major had both hands on the pistol directed straight at Milligan's grass-covered head. 'Arrest this man, he appears to be in some disguise.'

'It's all right,' said MacGillikudie, realizing the truth, 'It's Dan Milligan, he's all right.'

'What the hell was he hiding for, then?'

'He says what the hell was you hiding for, Milligan?'

'I was havin' a sleep, Sarge.'

'He says he was having a sl –'

'I can understand what he's saying!' shouted the Major, 'tell the idiot to be more careful in future.' The Major marched off, carelessly thrusting his pistol into the holster. There was a shot, a scream, and the Major took to clutching his foot and leaping. From nowhere the nobbly brown dog came snapping at his seat. What a noble sight. Man, beast and clutched foot, all leaping in perfect harmony. It was a great day for the Irish.

It was a greater one for the Jews. To Doctor Goldstein they took the wounded man. Laying on a stretcher, Stokes saw the nose of Goldstein hovering above.

'I say,' he said, momentarily forgetting his pain, 'You're a Jew. I don't want any damn Jew operating on me. Take me to a white man.'

'There's no other doctor for fifty miles and unless that bullet is removed you'll bleed to death!'

'Very well, then,' snapped the Major. 'Just this once then!'

Goldstein naturally knew of anti-Semitism. It was the most pleasant operation the doctor had ever performed. Without an anaesthetic.

Chapter Six

Sunday. Father Rudden clutched the pulpit. He had said mass at such a speed, the congregation were thrown into great confusion, some were standing, others kneeling, some were leaving, the rest gave up and sat down. Skipping the sermon he launched into a secular attack on the new border. 'If that border is to be permanent, it means that the Holy Catholic departed will forever be lying in British soil. *Protestant* soil, out there!!' He pointed in the wrong direction and dropped his voice.

'I should like for you who *all* feel strongly about this,' he raised his voice '*and you'd better*,' he crashed his fist down on the pulpit rail, splitting the wood and evicting a colony of woodlice; he lowered his voice, 'sign the petition you will find hanging in the foyer.' He stepped down, 'Dominus vobiscum,' he said, 'Et cum spirito tuo,' they replied. The verger counted the collection. 'It's a miracle how some of dese people's clothes don't fall off,' he grumbled, extricating the buttons from the plate.

Three miles away Dr Goldstein pulled the sheet over the face of Dan Doonan. Mrs Doonan took the news dry-eyed. She'd only stayed with him for the money. Twenty years before she had tried to get a separation. The solicitor listened to her attentively. 'But Mrs Doonan, just because you don't like him, that's no grounds for separation.'

'Well, make a few suggestions,' she said.

'Has he ever struck you?'

'No. I'd kill him if he did.'

'Has he ever been cruel to the children?'

'Never.'

'Ever left you short of money, then?'

'No, every Friday on the nail.'

'I see.' The solicitor pondered. 'Ah, wait, think hard now, Mrs Doonan, has he ever been unfaithful to you?'

Her face lit up. 'By God, I tink we got him there, I know for sure he wasn't the father of me last child!'

The solicitor had advised her accordingly. 'Get out of my office,' he told her and charged six and eight-pence for the advice.

Now Dan was dead. 'I wonder how much he's left me,' the widow wondered. Money couldn't buy friends but you got a better class of enemy.

Messrs Quock, Murdle, Protts and Frigg, solicitors and Commissioners for Oaths, pondered dustily over the grey will papers; at 98, Dan Doonan had died leaving all his money to himself. The quartet of partners shook their heads, releasing little showers of legal dandruff. They had thumbed carefully through the 3,000 pages of *Morell on Unorthodox Wills*, and no light was cast on the problem. Murdle took a delicate silver Georgian snuff box from his waistcoat, dusted the back of his hand with the fragrant mixture of Sandalwood and ground Sobrani, sniffed into each nostril, then blew a great clarion blast into a crisp white handkerchief.

'This will take years of work to unravel,' he told his companions; 'we must make sure of that,' he added with a sly smile, wink, and a finger on the nose. They were, after all, a reputable firm built up on impeccable business principles, carefully doctored books and sound tax avoidance.

Only the last paragraph of the said will was clear. Doonan wanted a hundred pounds spent on a grand 'Wake' in honour of himself. Senior partner, Mr Protts, stood up, drew a gold engraved pocket watch to his hand, snapped it closed, '4.32 exactly, gentlemen – Time for Popeye,' he said switching on the T.V.

The inebriated chanting of professional mourners came wailing from 44 Cloncarragah Terrace. Inside the front room, propped by the fireplace, was the flower-bedecked coffin of Dan Doonan. Grouped around admiringly, reverently clutching their drinks, were friends and foes alike, and with drink they were all very much alike. Funeral clichés were flying in the teeth of the dear departed.

'A fine man, ma'am, it's a great day for him.'

'You must be proud of him, Mrs Doonan.'

'One of the finest dead men ter ever walk the earth.'

'I was sorry ter see him go!'

'So was I – he owed me a pound.'

'It's hard to believe he's dead.'

'Oh he's *dead* is he?' said Foggerty, who'd been speaking to him all evening.

The corpse looked fine, fine, fine. New suit, hair cut and greased, his boots highly polished and loaned by an anonymous donor were firmly nailed to the coffin for additional security. The tables in the next room were swollen high with the food. Two wooden tubs steamed with baked potatoes, their earthy jackets split and running with rivulets of melting butter. Hot pig slices, a quarter inch thick, were piled high on seventeen plates. In the middle, was one huge dish of brown pork sausages, and bacon, still bubbling from the pan. On the floor, floating in a bucket of vinegar, was a minefield of pickled onions. The temporary bar was serving drinks as fast as O'Toole could pour them.

'God, there hasn't been a night like this since the signing of the Treaty.'

Many people die of thirst but the Irish are born with one.

O'Connor the piper tucked his kilt between his legs, puffed the bladder of his pipes and droned them into life; soon the floor was lost in a sea of toiling, reeling legs. Uppity-hippity-juppity-ippity-dippity-dippity shook the house. The centre bulb danced like a freshly hanged man. There was a clapping a stamping-and-cries-of-encouragement. The faithful few in Dan's parlour soon deserted him for the dance. Alone in his room he stood, his body jerking to the rhythm now shaking the house. The party was swelled by the arrival of the victorious Puckoon Hurley team, many still unconscious from the game. These were dutifully laid on the floor beside Dan's coffin – the rest joined into the frenzied dance.

The Milligan pulled his trousers up and leaped into the middle, but he observed his legs and stopped. 'Hey, you said me legs would develop with the plot.'

'They will.'

'Den why are they still like a pair of dirty old pipe cleaners?'

'It's a transitional period.'

'Look, I don't want transitional legs.' He stood in the middle of the leaping bodies and spoke, 'What's dis book all about, here we are on page-page – ' he looked down, 'on page 74 – and all these bloody people comin' and goin', where's it all going to end?'

'I don't know. Believe me, I'm just as worried as you are.'

'Tell me why? – tell me – give me a sign!'

A bottle bounced off Milligan's head.

'The Queen,' he shouted and fell sideways like a poleaxed ox.

Three fights had broken out in the midst of the dancers but the difference was hard to tell. The whole house now trembled from roof to foundations. In the next room the great family bible shook from the shelf above the coffin and struck Dan Doonan, throwing him from the coffin and catapulting him from his boots. His wig, a life-long secret, shot from his head and slid under the table next to the cat. He fell among the unconscious members of the Hurley team, who were starting to recover. 'He's drunk as a lord,' they said, dragging him across the hall and tucking him in bed.

'Good God, look at the size of that rat,' one said, seeing the cat pass with a wig in its jaws. 'He mustha' put up a fight.'

Placing a bottle of whisky by the bed they drank it and stumbled from the room.

It was 4.32 in the morning as the crow flies. The last mourners had slobbered out their drunken farewells, their voices and great posterior blasts mingling into the night. Mrs Doonan drained an empty bottle, scratched her belly, and made for her bed.

Somewhere in the night, Milligan, drunk and with lumps on his head, was wandering through the braille-black countryside: in his path a carefully written well. Splash! it went on receipt of his body.

At 4.56 in the morning, the quietly patrolling constable Oaf was reduced to a kneeling-praying holy man by a leg-weakening shriek. The door of number 33 burst open and out screamed Mrs Doonan in unlaced corsets.

'There's a man in me bed, get him out!' she yelled, restraining her abounding bosoms.

'Madame, if you can't frighten him in that get up, I certainly can't!'

'Do yer duty,' she said, ladelling her bosoms back.

The constable unclipped his torch, took a firm grip on his truncheon and entered the house.

'In that room,' she whispered.

'Leave him to me,' said Oaf, pushing her in front. He shone his torch on the bed. Mrs Doonan gasped and let fall her bosoms. 'Holy Mary!' she gasped, 'It's me husband.'

She fainted, clutching the policeman's legs as she fell, bringing his trousers to the ground. Now then, who would have thought a constable would use green knotted string for garters, and have red anchors tattooed on his knees? Ah, Ireland is still a land of mystery.

'Helpppp!' shouted Milligan from the bottom of the well. 'Helppp – pppp – pelp – elp – lp – ' it echoed up.

'Who's down there drinkin' me water?' A white face peered down the cool shaft. It was Farmer O'Mara.

'It's meeeee.'

'I know it's you, yer idiot! but what's yer name?'

'Milligan.'

'Dan? What you doin' down there, man?'

'I'm playing the cello. What do you think?'

He threw Milligan a rope. 'Hold tight.' O'Mara was a giant of a man, his hands hung from his shirtsleeves like raw hams. He started to pull. 'God, he's strong,' thought Milligan, ascending draggletail from his watery bower.

Drying out by the fire, O'Mara gave him hot tea and whisky. They awaited the morning. In the leaping firelight Milligan saw O'Mara's face. His eyes were cups of sadness, and seemed far, far older than him. A smile on that face would look like a sin.

Milligan knew the story. O'Mara had married a raving beauty, Sile Kerns. When he started courting her every man in the village had been through her, every one in the village knew it, all except O'Mara. Him being so big they were frightened to cast aspersions on the girl. The marriage bore three children, Sean, Laura and Sarah. It seemed that at last Sile had left her old ways behind her. Then O'Mara had

caught her red-handed, the lover had fled across the countryside without his trousers which were shown as evidence. O'Mara was awarded custody of the kids. That seemed the end of it, things settled down, all but Sile, who was slowly going out of her mind.

Losing the kids had done it. One night Sile got in to their bedroom and cut their throats. She would have had O'Mara too but for the fact he couldn't sleep for the toothache. She was taken away and put in Gedstow Asylum. There she sat out her life, sitting and looking at a wall, sitting and looking at a wall, sitting and looking at a wall. . . . From a man who laughed and loved life, O'Mara was cut down to a walking dead. It was thirteen years since then. Unknown to anybody, he still kept the children's beds made up and every night slept with a teddy bear and a dolly clutched in his great hairy arms.

Now he bred horses. In the spring he'd watch the young rubber-legged foals racing through the sweet morning grass, and sometimes he could see three laughing children on their backs. They lay buried in the Churchyard of St Theresa. He comforted himself with whisky, and an eternal hatred of women. 'You drink too much,' Dr Goldstein told him.

'Drink too much for what?' he asked in reply. The doctor, knowing his tragedy, stayed silent.

Sgt Joseph MacGillikudie read and re-read the official report. 'Is this all true?' he asked the blinking constable.

'It's just as it happened, Sarge.'

MacGillikudie removed his pince-nez. 'It's a

mystery then how did Dan Doonan get out of his coffin, take his boots off and get into bed without a wig on, at the same time being stone dead.' MacGillikudie thought towards the floor, and tapped the pince-nez on his thumb. 'Fancy! Him wearing a wig? I've known Doonan, man, woman and boy, for thirty years and never did I know he had the baldness. He must have been a master of disguise.' He closed the dossier and stamped it 'Unsolved'. Constable Oaf coughed, blinked and spoke.

'Technically speaking, Sarge, coming back to life is no crime.'

'Oh yes it is! If you come back, for a start you need a birth certificate. Meantime supposin' yer wife married again? What then? Eh? What then?'

'You can have her for bigamy,' smiled the Constable.

MacGillikudie waved him away. 'No, no, no, it's all wrong, bugger off!'

That night, wearing a cheap smoking jacket cut from blankets that his wife had made and laughed at, he lay in bed fuming and meditating. Crime! It obsessed him. When he joined the police he had destined himself for the high office of Chief Detective Inspector. After nearly twenty-seven years he was still eighteen promotions short. How could the Inspector have overlooked him for so long?

Of course, he *had* made mistakes. Like Dr Crippen. 'It looks like he did it,' MacGillikudie said, three days after the man had been hung. Nevertheless, there was no one alive who could match him for scientific criminological deduction. Fu Manchu, Sexton Blake,

Charlie Chan, he'd read them all, he'd learned the hard way – paperbacks. The lights went out, his wife settled beside him. 'Good night, Sherlock Holmes,' she said, laughing hysterically. One day, he thought, *one* day. He clenched and unclenched his fists under the bedclothes.

Chapter Seven

The funeral of Dan Doonan came treacle-slow from the church. 'Benedictus Deus, et pater Domini nostri Jesus Christi, Pater misericordium et deus' ... chanted Father Rudden, walking on ahead. As long as he said something in the Latin they all thought they were getting value for money. As a young priest it bothered him that the faithful never took the trouble to learn the meaning of Latin prayers. As a test, and under the influence of an overdose of whisky he had intoned the whole of a dirty story in Latin, which concluded with a solemn 'Amen' from the congregation.

They approached the new Border Customs Post. From a hut, a-buttoning his coat came Barrington.

'Good morning,' he said in those uneasy Civil Servants tones; not so much a greeting to the day as a farewell to personal liberty.

'A few formalities sir,' he continued, thrusting the Customs card at the priest. 'Read that, will you?'

'We have nothing to declare, sir, this is a funeral.'

'What have you got in the coffin?'

'You must be joking,' said the priest, his face going purple with anger, and his anger going white with rage.

'I'm *not* joking sir, I am merely doing my duty.'

'Very well. Inside the coffin is the body of 98-year-old Dan Doonan. Now let us pass!'

'Not quite finished yet, sir. You intend to bury an Irish citizen in what is now *British* territory?'

'That is true.'

The delay brought cries from the procession.

'Hurry up, it's goin' ter rain.'

'Get a move on before annuder of us passes on.'

'I got bad legs, mister.'

Barrington waited patiently, then continued.

'I presume the deceased will be staying this side permanently?' 'Unless someone invents a remarkable drug – yes,' answered the priest. 'Then,' went on Barrington, 'he will require the following: an Irish passport stamped with a visa, to be renewed annually for the rest of his – ' Barrington almost said 'life' – 'stay', he concluded.

Everyone was seeing red except Foggerty who was colour blind.

The priest's dark eyes were fixed on the composed face of his tormentor. Vengeance belongs to God, he thought, but this fellow belongs to me. Still staring at Barrington, the priest addressed the mourners:

'Take him back to the church, lads – we'll have to postpone the burial.'

The pall-bearers made a clumsy about turn and returned to the church. A wind was blowing up. The women held their black skirts and hats. The dust skirled along the road, looking for eyes to blink. Inside his box Dan Doonan was above it all.

Arthur Manuel Faddigan hummed 'The Rose of Tralee', screwed the top of his pile ointment, and pulled up his trousers. The photographic trade in

Ireland had been hard hit since the migration to America. Only the mad Mrs Bridie Chandler from the great ruined farm on the moor ever sat for him. Once a week she came galloping up, a great mountain of fat astride a black stallion; sweeping into the studio she'd strip off her clothes and shout 'Take me!' The first time had been shock enough. Faddigan had run all the way to church.

'Father,' he gasped, 'is it wrong to look at naked women?'

'Of course it is,' said Rudden, 'otherwise we'd all be doing it.' He had finally given Faddigan a dispensation to photograph her, providing he kept at a respectable distance.

Faddigan never did work out how much that was in feet and inches, and he never did comprehend 'How a woman could spread out in so many directions at once and still stay in the same place.'

His wife arrived one day when he was printing the negatives and beat him silly with a bottle of best developing fluid at 23 shillings a pint. 'You dirty pornographer,' she said, and left him for good. The small green shop bell tinkled briefly, and in came three men with the dangling Dan Doonan.

'Is he drunk?' inquired Mr Faddigan.

'No, no,' said one of Dan's supporters, 'he's got leg trouble.'

'What's his head hangin' down for?'

'He's got leg trouble right up to his neck.'

'Oh. Just sit him in the chair.' Doonan slid to the floor. 'Ups-a-daisy,' said Faddigan kindly.

'We want passport photos.'

'Is he going away then?'

'Yes.'

'Where to?'

'We're not sure, but he's got a choice of two places.'

'Just hold him like that, I can see he's an old man. Smileeee.... There, that's it. If he's pleased with the result, perhaps he'll come again.'

'Oh, he'll never be that pleased,' said the departing trio. And they carried dear Dan away.

Autumn laid a russet hand over the county. The great summer trees cried their leaves to the ground; dead, hollow spiders clung transparently to once geometric webs; swallows enumerate on wires; the golden penny that was the sun devalued. Wan shafts of sunlight struck Puckoon like old ladies' uncertain fingers. The fox went farther afield, his coat thicker, his stomach thinner; the seasons were on their endless march and the North wind was greening the tree trunks. 'Tank God the grass has stopped growin',' Milligan said, as he greased the scythes for their long hibernation. 'Oh dear, dear, dear! Is this the age of the common man?' If so, no one regretted it more than the common man himself. Who was the common man? You point to anybody and say, 'You are the common man,' and you'd get punched in the nose. Liberation from slavery! That was the cry from Wat Tyler to Castro. What a lot of cock! *Any* man is willing to become a slave, as long as he was paid enough. There was no such thing as *anything*, and sometimes even less.

'Hello, dere.'

Milligan looked to the voice. It was the black-coated Foggerty wandering aimlessly along outside the church wall, eating an unpeeled banana. 'I'm on me way to the meetin'. You coming?'

'The meeting? Good God, I forgot! That's right.' Milligan rushed into his overcoat and made quickly for the Church Hall, on his bike, Foggerty running alongside.

'Why you holding your head, Milligan?'

'I got a headache.'

'Don't come near me den,' cautioned Foggerty, 'I don't want to catch it.'

The dead leaves scattered before the two men. 'I suppose,' thought Milligan, 'now the grass has gone, the next job will be the leaves, Nature works hand in glove against the likes of me.' Bein' alive didn't give you a moment's rest. He felt his legs. They were as thin as ever.

The corrugated iron roof of the Puckoon Church Hall reverberated to the angry shouts within. Every now and then little cakes of rust fell free and settled on the heads of the assembled. It was a very important meeting. The whole of Puckoon was there; the front bench was packed to a fifth full, the flag of the Republic nailed bravely to the wall behind the Speakers' rostrum.

'We're not going to put up wid dis,' said Mrs O'Brien. 'Every time I want ter visit me father's grave I have to be searched by the customs man and,' she added, 'he's got cold hands. On top of that, I got to show a passport of meself.'

Down she sat.

Up she stood.

'It's a disgrace.'

Up she stood, down she sat, 'I've had enough of it!' She whacked her umbrella down flush on the recumbent head of Mrs Ellis. Up *she* stood. 'Ohhh!' she screamed. Down sat Mrs O'Brien, up stood Father Rudden waving a calming hand, 'Steady now, steady, I know how you all feel. Can we continue with further complaints in relation to the new frontier?'

Mr Murtagh, stinking town clerk and amnesic, arose with a sheaf of closely typed quarto papers, removed his reading glasses and began to read.

'Ahem! Report of an accident on the Ballyshag Bridge over the River Puckoon. As we all know this bridge has been divided in two by an unthoughtful boundary commission.'

There were three cries of 'Shame!' and one of 'Bastards!'

Last week, a motor car containing a driver and a charabanc of old pensioners were in collision. The car finished on the Ulster side of the border and the charabanc on ours. As a result the case was being held in two countries at once. Witnesses were rushed by high-powered car from court to court to give evidence and they weren't getting any younger. The driver of the charabanc, a Mr Norrington, a retired English actor, had been thrown from his driving seat, his body laying athwart the border; now his legs were being sued by the passengers of the charabanc, and his top half was claiming damages from the car driver.

The solicitors predicted that the case would last three years because of the travel involved. Murtagh concluded with a flourish of his papers. 'Any more?' asked the priest, peering around. 'No?'

'Yes!' Mr O'Toole jumped to his feet. 'This boundary affects me, terribly. My pub is all in this side of the border, all except two square feet in the far corner of the public bar.'

'Is that a hardship?' asked Father Rudden.

'Is it? That two square feet is in Ulster, where the price of drinks is thirty per cent cheaper. Now, every night, me pub is empty, save for a crowd of bloody skinflints all huddled in that corner like Scrooges.'

Father Rudden promised a solution and closed the meeting.

With Rafferty's weight on the cross bar, Milligan pedalled home from the meeting via the Holy Drinker. They had tried to get into the cheap corner but were crowded out. But never mind, no matter what price you paid for liquor, it always tasted better.

'My lord, you're heavy,' Milligan grumbled.

'Don't ferget half of it is you, Milligan.'

'I'm only complaining about *your* half, which after all is the biggest.'

'Well, I'm grateful for the lift, Milligan.'

'With you holding me by the throat, I had no option.'

'It's just my way of askin'.'

A lemon-peel moon rose into the cold sky. Milligan whistled.

'Dat's a nice tune.'

'It's part of the Eroica Symphony – I wrote it.'

'*You* write the Eroica?'

'Yes.'

'What about Beethoven?'

'Yes, I wrote that as well.'

'You bloody liar.'

Cheerfully he whistled his next composition, Grieg's A Minor Concerto by Milligan. Life wasn't too bad. The trouble with Man was, even while he was having a good time, he didn't appreciate it. Why, thought Milligan, this very moment might be the happiest in me life. The very thought of it made him miserable.

Still, he had known happier times. To be born in India the son of a Sergeant-Major in the Indian Army, that was a different start from the other boys.

Living in India those days was something. People who had been hungry unemployed farm labourers in Ireland were suddenly unemployed N.C.O.'s in the British Army, with real live servants of their own. The first house he remembered was 5 Climo Road, Poona. Built after the Indian mutiny, the walls were white-washed and the ceiling was a tightly stretched canvas. At night young Dan would watch the tracks of the mice as they scurried across it. The front of the house was half trellis and half wall. A corrugated iron canopy stretched out from the roof to hold back the sun. In the monsoons the water thundered on to the iron sheets and made it sound like a different world. What wonderful days they were, full of golden dreaming, where nothing matters except 'now', everything was always in *now*, tomorrow was no good until it became *now*, and as there appeared to be an endless supply of now, nothing else mattered. The whole family lived together; Grandmother, bed-ridden Grandad, Aunty Eileen, Uncle Hughie. He had developed a craze for the saxophone and body building. He managed to combine the two. Stripping to the waist, wearing a pair of underpants painted to look like leopard skin, he stood in front of a mirror, playing Valse Vanity and doing knees bend. He was quick to discover that pressing certain notes on the saxophone brought various muscles into play. For instance, bottom E flat showed the right bicep to advantage, middle C alternating with bottom C brought the pectorals into play.

More complicated combinations followed. Lying flat playing middle C fortissimo and arching his back from the legs gave prominence to the lines of the abdominal ridge. Holding the saxophone above the head, bending backwards and playing repetitive B sharps, showed the deltoids in all their flexed glory. From this simple beginning, a unique idea was to formulate. For two years he worked on it in absolute secrecy. It turned out to be a Concerto for Alto-Saxophone and Human Muscles. Full of zeal he entered the work in an amateur talent contest at the West End Cinema, Poona. Pouring with sweat and blowing notes in all directions, he was watched in mystified silence by a baffled Hindu audience. After twenty minutes of grunting strainings he was booed from the stage. He later sold the idea to a travelling Armenian herbalist who, with delusions of grandeur, tried to curry favour by performing it before the

Czarina, but he was shot by a palace guard whilst trying to invade her bedchamber.

Then there was 'Soap' Holloway. The favourite trick they played on him was talking him into messing his pants, then telling his mother. One evening 'Soap' fell out of a nim tree. He lay there very quiet. 'Come on, you'll be all right,' young Dan said.

'He's not breathing,' said a kid.

They ran and told his mother. The last they saw of 'Soap' was his father carrying him at the double, his mother running alongside crying and saying something. It didn't matter what, 'Soap' wasn't one of them any more. On hot nights, Dan's mother would move his bed into the small garden. He would lie there, looking at the sky through the mosquito net.

There was the Plough – that one was easy. The rest could go to hell. He would fall asleep to the peculiar smell of the nim tree and the distant chug-chug of the engine that lit the Empire Cinema.

Poona had one of the finest race courses in India. At the height of the season it was the thing to belong to the Western India Turf Club. At an early age Milligan got the taste for horses and betting. With a rupee pocket money he'd enjoy the meeting from the middle of the course. The stands were a riot of colour. Pugrees, saris, white dhotis, there was the Maharajah of Kolapur in orange silk trousers, syces in white with polished brass shoulder trappings led in the horses, the Aga Khan, then a young man with many wives to go. Everywhere the smell of betel-nut and pan biddy.

Milligan remembered his first bet with a short Hindu bookie who wrote his betting slips on rice paper so in case of raids they could be eaten. It was the Governor's Cup, the Derby of India. Milligan had picked out 'Cherrio', a pure white Arab horse, a Pegasus without wings. She sailed home. Milligan ran for his winnings only to find the Hindu bookie under arrest. Charged with molesting an Indian woman between races, he had protested he had never touched the woman. She said he had but she hadn't minded it. Apparently it was the policeman who was jealous and broke up the fun.

Those days were all gone. It might never have happened.

'You've gone quiet, Milligan,' said Rafferty, now three stone heavier.

'No Irishman can enjoy himself alone for long, Rafferty. I was thinkin' of me boyhood.'

Suddenly Rafferty went tense. 'I think we're on the wrong road, Milligan.'

'Why d'you say that?'

'We've just passed a Chinaman.'

'We couldn't have come *that* far.'

'I'm not joking. It was a Chinee, I tell you, not only that, he was wearing a policeman's hat.'

'We never had that much to drink, did we?'

They argued into the beckoning night. From the roadside, Constable Lee Ah Pong made a note of two drunken men arguing on a bike. He looked at his watch and then added the time to his report. He waxed mysterious and disappeared sideways into the dark.

Ah Pong of Peking, China, had arrived in Dublin on a tramp steamer *The General Gordon*, engaged in smuggling monkeys from India to Tilbury. The

Scottish Captain Gordon MacThun had lost his way many times before. Last year he set course for Madras and arrived at Elba. As Ah Pong remarked, 'Scotsman doesn't know his Madras from his Elba.' The little Chinese had done the trip to escape the stark poverty of China and was soon happily walking in the stark poverty of Ireland. He had jumped ship in Dublin with his worldly fortune of twelve pounds in yens. The money was pre-Czarist and was in several stages of devaluation at the same time. It took a Dublin bank clerk eighteen hours and two mental breakdowns to work out the exchange. Ah Pong came out with a smile and asked the first stranger:

'Hello General Gordon, where China Town?'

Not having one, the Dubliner thought the next best thing would be the Jewish quarter. He took Ah Pong to Frogg Street and pointed to a sign 'Bed and Breakfast for hire.' A large woman opened a small door.

'You want a room?' Mrs Goldberg asked.

'Please, I not make English much, hello – I come lite out Peking. Oh hello – General Gordon. Me.'

'I don't know what he's sayin',' she shouted back down the passage. 'I think its General Gordon,' she added.

'Wot is it?' Mr Goldberg came blinking-shuffling up the corridor. 'Oh,' he saw Ah Pong. 'He's all right, he's a Foreigner, they eat *anything*. Come in, come in.' He made a friendly gesture with the Dublin *Jewish Chronicle*. 'You a tourist then?'

'Me Chinee.'

'Oh, you a Chinee? Well, well. We live and learn, eh? How's Sun Yat Sen gettin' on?'

'Cup of tea, Mr Chinese?' asked Mrs Goldberg, removing the cost.

Ah Pong made a sign in mime that he wished a bed for the night, lying on the floor and placing his hands along his head.

'See that, Rachel,' said the enlightened Mr Goldberg, 'Chinese drink it lying down.'

A puzzled Chinee watched as both Goldbergs took his tea stretched on the floor. Lodgers were hard to come by, and at all costs to be encouraged.

A true son of the Orient, Ah Pong carried his customs with him. The Chinese New Year came. 'Happy New Year,' he shouted to a tram full of puzzled Dubliners and was bodily hurled off. For weeks he had searched for employment. His little store of money soon dwindled. One day he told the Goldbergs, 'Hello. Goodbye. Me I money all gone. No work here for Chinee. I bugger off, General Gordon.'

The Goldbergs had grown very fond of the little man. He paid his rent on the dot and didn't mind chickens in his bedroom. Mr Goldberg remembered the new Republic was desperately short of policemen. They had advertised the fact in *The Sligo Clarion* – '*Men of good physique over 4 ft 3 ins. will find a good life in the new Irish Free State Police Force.*'

Inspector Gogarty Muldoon was hard put to it. He parry-diddled a pencil on his desk. 'A Chinee,' he kept muttering and looking out the window. 'God knows we need recruits ... but a Chinee?' He stood up. A fine wreck of a man dissipated by a thousand nights of debauchery, he had obtained his present position by sending his immediate superior an April fool telegram. 'All is known,' that's all it said. The effect was startling. His superior had fled the country and was now a Sanitary Inspector in Madrid. The current shortage of men was Muldoon's only worry. Blinking at him was the pneumatic face of Sgt Behan.

'He's a nice little feller, sir,' he said.

'Nice, yes, Behan, but consider the prospect. If Ah Pong becomes a constable he's bound to succeed, as the Chinese are very clever. I read that. Now – ' the Inspector pulled the lobe of his nose, ' – he'll write to his relations in Peking and tell them that there is jobs over here with uniforms, lodgings, pay and allowances.' He looked at Behan. 'Don't you see, Sergeant? If Ah Pong gets in, ten years from now the entire police force of Ireland would be Chinese.'

'Including me?' asked the worried sergeant.

The Inspector didn't reply. 'We could make him a policeman if there's a quiet out-of-the-way post ter send him, and bring the Irish constable back to Dublin where he is needed.' He looked at the wall map.

'Hmnn. Sergeant, bring me the constabulary strength of Puckoon.'

'Right, sir,' Behan issued smartly from and back to the room.

The Inspector turned the pages. 'Heavens alive! We're supposed to have a police strength of five out there and there's only two left. What's happened to the other three?'

'Six years for assault and battery, sir!'

'That's the place then. We'll train Ah Pong and then send him up there.'

At 4.32 on the stroke of midnight, 7 dedicated men sat around a table in the vestry of St Theresa.

'Men,' began Father Rudden, looking at the faces of O'Mara, O'Brien, Milligan, Rafferty and Dr Goldstein. 'I think you all know why we're here.'

They nodded their heads, some grunted, Milligan said 'Yes.'

'Good,' said Rudden. 'The trouble is this. Three people from Puckoon have to go through that Customs gate to see their departed. Those are the graves of – ' he read from a small piece of paper ' – Patrick Grogan, Harold O'Lins and Dan Doonan. God rest their souls. So – ' he sucked his breath through his teeth ' – unpleasant as I find it, I feel obliged to remove their bodies from that side for reburial over here. This can only be achieved by asking *their* permission – ' he pointed towards the Customs '– *which I resent*! Or bring them back secretively under cover of darkness. I favour the latter.'

'Which is the latter, Father?' said Milligan.

'That's the under cover of darkness one. I have devised an infallible plan, which *mustn't* fail.'

The brass stare of the oil lamp suffused the room, the faces of the plotters bathed yellow in the tallow light. The priest outlined his plan and swore them all to secrecy.

'Before you go,' said Father Rudden, 'let's drink a toast!' He took a bottle of unblessed communion wine from the cupboard. 'Beaujolais,' he said phonetically, '1920, a good year.'

'Be a better year when you open it, Father.'

'Patience, Milligan, patience.'

Patience, thought Milligan, that word was invented by dull buggers who couldn't think quick enough.

'Now then,' the priest was saying, 'wine must be treated with respect.' So saying, he shook the bottle violently. 'Mix all the goodness in,' he said gleefully.

Goldstein's Bacchanalian soul withered at the barbarities being meted out to the royal and most sensitive liquid known to men. Red Burgundy. He couldn't remember how long he had loved wine, but Red Burgundy had been his mistress since he was eighteen.

Year after year his father, the late Ben Tovim Goldstein, had laid down wines in the little cellar under their house. Not being well off, the wine was usually only served on holidays. And such a fuss was made of it. Even in the frugal rationing days of the war, when they had a house in North Finchley, even with such food as tinned grade three Russian salmon, Poppa Goldstein would fuss along in the kitchen, making momma add this and that. The salmon would be cooked in cheap white Algerian wine and a hot mayonnaise sauce poured over the top. New potatoes grown on the allotment were French fried slightly brown and dusted with cheese at the last moment. Poppa would bring it in to his five hungry children with a great deal of noise and a good deal of rhetoric.

'Caught this morning in a Scottish river and especially flown down by the R.A.F.,' he would say.

'Now, with this entree, what do we drink?'

'White!' chorused his indoctrinated children.

'Yes, white,' he would beam.

He would then take the white from a small ice bucket and feel it.

'Hmm,' he would murmur, looking pensively at the ceiling, 'Forty degrees, just right,' and he would pinch his thumb and forefinger together and kiss it away. He made much of wrapping a clean serviette around the neck of the bottle. 'White Burgundy 1937, Chateau bottled, and imported by Mr Patrick Ford of London, who only bought at the candle light sales.'

Now he would spill a little in a Paris goblet, and swirl it around, every now and then tilting the glass forward and savouring it with his nose.

'When you are accustomed to it, you can tell by the bouquet *exactly* whether you are going to like it or not. The taste comes second, but that is usually just a confirmation of what your nose has already decided.'

Here he sipped. 'As I thought! A little young, better in another two years, but still delightful.'

He would pour them all a 'Damp Glass' as he called it. 'The older you are the more you get, so hurry up and grow.'

They would all clink glasses and chorus 'Lechayim'.

Then the meat course and with it the red, round-bodied, luscious Burgundy.

'Chambertin 33,' said Poppa. 'Liquid velvet grown just South of Dijon.'

Just after breakfast Poppa would go down into the cellar and bring up one precious bottle. The war was on, France had capitulated, and no more red was coming into the country. After four hours he would decant, and then stand the green glass decanter in the dining room.

'Idiots laugh at this ritual,' he would say, 'but we Oneophiles know how to get the best from the wine.'

Father would hold the first glass of red up to the light and carefully examine it for sediment and colour.

'Poppa, what was the greatest meal ever served?'

Poppa puzzled at young Sean's question.

'The greatest I don't know but –' here he closed his eyes and put his finger on his nose. Suddenly he spoke. 'The meal served at the Tuilleries in 1820, I have a copy in my wallet, listen to this; no, better still, I will read you the most extraordinary menu, which proves that the French under no matter what harrowing conditions still attain the heights of civilization.' Poppa donned his glasses and read.

'Dinner served at the Cafè Voisin, 261 Rue Saint-Honorè, on December 25th 1870, 99th day of the siege.'

Here he looked around to observe their surprise, then continued.

Hors D'oeuvres
Butter-Radishes, Stuffed Donkey's Head, Sardines

Soups
Purée of Red Beans with Croûtons
Elephant Consommé

Entrées
Fried Gudgeons, Roast Camel English Style
Jugged Kangaroo
Roast Bear Chops au Poivre

Roasts
Haunch of Wolf, Venison Sauce
Cat Flanked by Rats
Watercress Salad
Antelope Terrine with Truffles
Mushroom Bordelaise
Buttered Green Peas

Dessert
Rice Cake with Jam
Gruyère Cheese

Wines

(Here Poppa's face beamed)

First service
Sherry
Latour Blanche 1861!
Château Palmer 1864!

'Now *second* service,' he emphasized:

Mouton Rothschild 1846!
Romanee Conti 1858!
Grand Porto 1827!

He folded the paper, and patted his brow where an excitement of perspiration had grown. They gathered by the menu that the Paris Zoo had been held in reserve for a Christmas Dinner. At the time young Sean was only seven, and the names of the great wine Chateaus that his father rolled off meant very little to him, but his father's persistence had borne fruit and the whole family were now confirmed lovers of wine.

Right now, however, terrible things were happening. Father Rudden was pulling another cork to shreds and pouring the wine.

'Wine,' the priest was saying, 'is liquid Christianity, there was never a bigger argument against the teetotallers than the Miracle at Cana.' Five glasses clinked. 'Schlaunty!' they chorused. They all drank. They drank again. Then, several more agains, then a series of agains followed by one long permanent again. Father Rudden was starting to rock unsteadily. Laughter was coming more frequent, and an occasional song. The conversation got around to religion.

'I say,' said the suddenly enlightened Milligan, 'I say that Roman Catholicism is losin' ground.'

'Ha, Ha,' said the priest, 'losing ground? With 500 millions at the last count?' O'Brien rubbed his chin. 'That's the trouble, it's like commercial television, never mind what kind of audience you got as long as you got plenty of 'em. The world is only concerned with numbers, not quality. It's a biological fact that you can't have numbers *and* quality. All things that continue in numbers run to seed. If not to seed they become a commune of non-thinkers like ants or bees.'

The priest drained his glass. 'Rubbish!' he said, wiping his mouth. 'Catholicism is still a great power.'

'I don't think so Father. Look, the Catholic Missionaries were in China three hundred years before Communism, and now? Where are the Catholics in China today? Out! Finished!'

'We'll be back, you see.'

'Not without a war Father,' interjected Rafferty. 'And that's no way to get converts.'

Father was busy opening another bottle of wine, he spoke from the dark recess of the room.

'We'll have to wait and see, that's all that's left, wait

and see.' He reappeared with a fresh bottle. 'Before I open this one, I want to make an appeal. We are in need of a fighting fund to help us with accessories. I should like to start by asking for donations right now!'

There was a grim, long, embarrassing silence.

'Come, come, come? I'm not asking for hundreds of pounds, just a little to start with. Will someone say ten shillings?'

'I can say it, Father,' said Milligan, 'but I haven't got it.'

'I've got it,' thought Dr Goldstein, 'but I'm not going to say it.'

O'Brien had opened his wallet and without a word spread three one-pound notes on to the table in front of the priest.

'There, Father, that's for the lot of us, I had a good win at the races today.'

With his hand shaking, and silenced by the vastness of the amount, the Father picked up the money.

'God bless you, O'Brien, dis will cover everything.'

The glasses clinked again, the light from the lamp shone through the wine, and the ceiling was dancing with the leaping red rubies from below.

'This will have to be the last one, early Mass tomorrow, Schlaunty!' said the priest as he drained his glass, made the sign of the cross and fell backwards into the dark.

'Ah, the poor man's tired,' said O'Mara, picking the priest up and carefully placing him on his bed. Milligan removed the priest's shoes.

'God God,' said the Milligan, 'if I had dat many holes in me socks, I'd use 'em as mittens.'

Little did he know that the priest frequently did. Money! That was the trouble. Money!

Chorusing good nights to the sleeping priest, the five took the road home.

It was a high, crisp, starry night, lovers were locked warmly in their doorways, noiseless was the moon-mad sea. Merrily the five followed the road to Puckoon that streamed silver ahead of them. Gold-stein clung to O'Mara, O'Mara to Rafferty, Rafferty to O'Brien and O'Brien on to Milligan and his bike. This inebriated daisy chain stumbled forward. Although the general direction seemed to be forward, a lot of the time was taken in falling backwards and sideways; however, they were gradually making progress in all directions. Flanking the road was the dank dark of the Puckoon Woods.

'This is just the night for poaching,' said Rafferty. 'Come with me.' He turned them sharp into a ploughed field and made for the trees.

'I got a few rabbit traps along here and one big fox trap.'

'Do you use them torture traps, Rafferty?' asked O'Mara.

'Gins? God no. Only bastards use them. I makes me own, painless and the animal can't hurt itself. I sent the plans to the R.S.P.C.A., dere tinkin' about it.'

Milligan stumbled. 'Bugger – what's the R.S.P.C.A.?'

'Well,' said Rafferty, climbing a stile. 'It's supposed to be a society for the prevention of cruelty to animals, the idea is good, but I found that most of the people who join are dog lovers, that or cats, the rest of the animal kingdom can go to hell. Mind you, there are some real fine members.'

The boots of the revellers were now great puddings of clay and mud.

'How much farther?' gasped O'Brien.

'I got me traps all along der banks of the river in dem trees,' and he pointed off into the dark. Unsteadily they plodded towards the river, their travels interjected with drunken singing, frequent halts and bawdy laughter as some took to spraying the trees.

'For dis relief, much tanks, Horatio,' said Milligan, posturing and laughing hysterically.

Chapter Eight

GULIO CAESAR presents *The World's Finest Animal Circus*. The words were painted six foot high in modest black and white. Circus master Gulio Caesar, 'King of the Ring', was a worried man. Constantly at war with fleas that continually transferred their allegiance from the monkeys to him, he slept with a tin of Keatings by his bed. At midnight he awoke scratching and cussing, when through his caravan window he made the awful discovery. The cage was open and the beast had gone. Scratching with one hand and dialling with the other, he phoned the R.S.P.C.A.

Awakening from his veterinary slumbers, Inspector Felix Wretch groped in the dark for the jangling instrument.

'Hello?'

'This is a – Gulio Caesar, could I please spik wid your husband?'

'Me husband speaking,' said Mr Wretch.

'Gooda, one of my black-a panthers has escape.'

Mr Wretch gulped himself into consciousness. 'I'll meet you outside the police station right away in ten minutes.'

'Right,' the line clicked to immutability.

Hurriedly Mr Wretch pocketed a humane killer, a phial of liquid and a hypodermic, then stepped into his trousers and into the night.

Into the wood along the river bank stumbled five happy drunks. Suddenly Rafferty stopped.

'Shhh, there's something in me trap,' he said excitedly.

The information silenced the singing. Cautiously they approached towards a black sleek shape crouching on the ground.

'It's a –' commenced Rafferty, but was cut short by a scarlet mouth emitting an unusually loud growl. 'No, it isn't,' he concluded.

'It isn't what?' queried O'Brien.

'It isn't what I thought it was at first.'

'Oh?'

'It should,' went on Rafferty, peering at the creature, 'it should be a fox.' The creature repeated a growl loud enough to stop the five in their tracks. What it was they knew not, that it was very big they knew, but what type of big they also knew not.

'I don't tink it's a goat,' Milligan said.

'You're right,' agreed Dr Goldstein. 'It's the wrong noise for a goat, if it was a goat it would go –' (he drew a big breath) ' – BAAAAAAAAAAA, BA-AAAAAAAAAAAA.' 'For God's sake keep quiet, Doctor,' said Rafferty, who for the first time in his poaching life was puzzled.

'BBBBBBBBBBBBBBAAAAAAAAAAA!' continued Goldstein. Kneeling on all fours he charged O'Brien's unsuspecting seat.

'What in h –' O'Brien started to say as he fell forward. There was an inky black pause and a great splash. 'You bloody Jewish idiot!' said O'Brien, wallowing-groping-stumbling-falling in the shallow river waters. 'Gis yer hand,' said O'Mara pulling the soggy O'Brien to the bank.

'Feel if dere's any fish in his pockets,' said the Milligan holding his stomach with laughter.

'Shhhhhhhhhhh!' said Rafferty.

'I'll get you for dis, Goldstein,' said O'Brien. They were all silenced by a low, almost evil, snarl from the beast. Rafferty took a coil of rope from his sack. 'Here, little animal,' he said advancing cautiously. The reply was a stomach-loosening roar. Rafferty stopped uneasily and walked back to the arguing, singing group. 'A thought just struck me,' said Rafferty. 'Is dere any wild wolves left in Ireland?'

'Now I think I can answer that,' said Goldstein, 'Will someone strike a light?'

Milligan struck a match as the doctor read from a small pocket encyclopaedia, unsteadily flicking the pages.

'Ahhhhh!' he said. 'Listen, dere are no wild wolves left in Ireland. The last one was killed in 1785 in MacGillikudie's Reeks by a German naturalist called Herman Von Loon. Oh,' he read on, 'here's another bit of interesting data. In 1794 a black man called Talmadge Frock crossed Ireland on a wooden roller skate and died of leg cramps. He . . .'

Darkness followed a yell as the match burnt Milligan's finger.

'What about gettin' this animal, I'm gettin' cold,' O'Brien said.

Rafferty beckoned them all towards the beast. 'I'll get this noose over his neck, den everyone take one leg each.'

They advanced unsteadily. 'Puss, puss, puss,' said the Milligan, holding out his hand.

'You're right, Milligan, it's a cat, a black cat. Gad, he's had a good feed, look at the size of him.'

The animal sprang, uprooting the trap, hitting O'Mara in the chest. O'Mara the giant got to his feet.

'No bloody pussy-cat's going to do that to me.' He lashed out, struck the animal a pole-axe blow, and the panther sank into unconsciousness.

The five split up. O'Mara paused only once on the way, to throw a struggling panther into the charge room of the police station. There followed a series of ripping, growls and screams, then came a shattering of glass as the night constable dived through the window and ran up the road.

Two little men with the arse out of their trousers were holding a mass meeting. They had both known better days but not partaken in them. They were forced to admit that the glorious days of the I.R.A. were in decline.

'Comrades,' said Shamus Ford, addressing his partner from a chair, 'I have good tidings. This new Customs Post at Puckoon is a boon and a blessing to men. I have a plan, such a plan as Brian Boru would be glad to be associated in.'

Looking at him, adoringly, was the sad, middle-aged, unshaven little face of the faithful follower, Lenny Braddock. He scratched himself furiously, at the same time giving off a few supporting 'Hear hears'. Shamus banged his mittened hands across his body. The deserted barn was draughty, dirty, and dungy, but rent free. Shamus went on with great fire:

'To bury the stiffs dese days, they'se got to takes 'em through dat new Customs Post, it's a gift from heaven, don't you see?'

'No, I don't see, Shamus.'

'Pay attention den, gi's a puff on yer fag . . . ta . . . Our contacts on the other side says they're short of explosives. Right?'

'If you say so . . .'

'I do. Now normally, without the convenience of a coffin, you'd have yer luggage searched and yer pockets.'

'That's true, that's true . . . can I have me fag back?'

'Now. If we could get a coffin and rig up a phony burial, we could carry enough gelignite stuff in dat coffin to blow Ulster back into the Republic – you see?'

'Gor! By gor! Dat is a fine plan boyo! A fine plan! I tink this is a turning point in the history of Ireland. Can I have me fag back?'

'Wot we need is a coffin – don't snatch like that.'

'Me fag –'

'A coffin! Now, dere's a mortician in Delarose Street . . . you got them counterfeit pound notes? Good.'

'Can I have me fag back?'

'Of course, we got to make the plan watertight.' Shamus reclined back on his straw throne.

'Tomorrow I'll make arrangements fer der coffin.'

Suddenly, it was tomorrow. 'God, doesn't time fly?' said Shamus.

A recently lacerated constable with a finely shredded seat to his trousers addressed Mr Gulio Caesar. 'Have you lost a black panther, sir?'

'Yes, I have – she's-a-gone. Disastro!'

'I think I have made contact with the animal.'

The constable described his flight from fur-covered death. 'The animal is lurking in the wood a mile south of the church of St Theresa.'

'Mama mia! My porra panther – me and Mr Wretch will get there at a-once.'

'At once,' repeated Mr Wretch, loading his hypodermic.

They set off with a horse-drawn cage and a plentiful supply of drugged meat. It was dangerous for a panther to wander alone in Ireland. Once in paleolithic ages great dinatrons roamed the Celtic swamps. They had become extinct not of evolutionary process; there were O'Maras alive in those times, too.

In six months from recruitment, Ah Pong had picked up an amount of the language and could write a report on simple Irish crimes – murder, rape, etc. Kitted out in blue, he was given a warrant and entrained to Puckoon. Appearing at the door of Puckoon Police Station, he was arrested on sight.

'Constable Oaf, you've been drinking,' MacGillikudie had accused him.

'Me not Constable Oaf,' said the little Chinese.

'Then I arrest you for-for-you!' The accompanying

letter was hard to believe. From the Commissioner of Police? He must be off his nut! A Chinese policeman in exchange for Oaf? 'I don't suppose it's a bad swop,' he reflected.

He found Ah Pong a very willing worker, and therefore gave him the lot. Clever people these Chinese. Sax Rohmer had said so, he should know, he was one of them. He kept Ah Pong on night duty. He explained his reasons. 'Got to break it to the people gentlemanlike,' that and the other reason, a hungry panther loose.

The world had so many Chinese they wouldn't miss this one.

Passing the station one day, Rafferty had dropped in to see if there were any warrants out for his arrest. He entered. Ah Pong had his back to the door.

'Good morning, Sarge,' said Rafferty cheerfully.

Ah Pong turned. 'Please?' he said. The little Chinaman advanced towards Rafferty.

'Don't come near me MacGillikudie, I don't want to catch it.'

'Please, what-is-trouble?' said Ah Pong.

I was right, thought Rafferty, dat was a Chinee I saw the other night.

'Where's Sergeant MacGillikudie?' he asked.

'Sergeant asleep.'

'Does he know you're wearing his uniform?'

'Please understand, I real police, my name Ah Pong.'

He held out his hand and shook Rafferty's.

'You're a *real* polis?'

'Look.' Ah Pong put on his helmet, pointed one finger in the air, and blew his whistle. 'See?'

Rafferty paused, his lips pursed. His face took on a cunning look.

'Do you know the meaning of the word poacher?'

'Sorry, me no understand.'

Rafferty's face burst into a smile. 'Me and you is going to get on real fine.' He shook the smiling Chinaman's hand and departed. Ah Pong opened a Chinese-English dictionary and ran his finger down the Ps, P-O-A-C-H-E-R. Ahhhh!

He made a swift note in Pekinese. Soon Rafferty was to know the meaning of the word 'inscrutable'.

Chapter Nine

Life is a long agonized illness only curable by death. Ruben Croucher lovingly and delicately dusted the coffins displayed in his parlour. They were such beautiful things. Stately barques that bore us across the Styx into the eternal life beyond. All was peace and calm within. The only sound was the endless buzzing of a lone fly, who shall remain nameless. Ruben Croucher walked with crane-like dignity across the black cracking lino to the window. His long thin nose pointed the way; a million rivers of tiny ruptured veins suffused his cadaverous face, two watery eyes like fresh cracked eggs in lard looked out from a skull-like head. It had got dark early and he had lit the gas, which cast a sepulchral glow along the neatly arranged coffins. With a cloth he wiped the condensation from the sightless windows. Business was bad, it seemed people couldn't afford to die these days. But, what was this?

Two ragged-arsed men were approaching, both smoking the same cigarette. They were pulling a cart and heading rapidly for the shop. Pausing only to open the door, they entered. When Lenny saw the face of Mr Croucher, he reverently took his hat off. Croucher bowed ever so slightly from the waist up.

'Good morning,' he said, then after some thought added, 'Gentlemen.' After all they could be eccentric millionaires.

Shamus coughed. 'We are eccentric millionaires,' he said. 'Do you sell coffins?'

Mr Croucher nodded. 'Yes, we do, sir,' and as a try on, 'how many do you want?'

'Oh, just one to start with.'

'Good, good. Who is the deceased?'

'Oh.' Shamus hadn't thought of this, but he was a man of some guile. 'It's for me friend here,' and he pointed at Lenny. 'You see,' he went on, 'he hasn't been well lately, and we thought just to be on the safe side we'd have one now.' Mr Croucher, though puzzled, pressed on. 'Ahem. Well, I suppose this method will save normal post mortem mensuration.'

'Eh?'

'Measuring him. Now he can – well – try one for size.' Mr Croucher indicated the coffins. Shamus and Lenny ran their hands over several. 'We'll have that one.' Shamus pointed.

'Ah, a black one. A very wise choice, sir, it won't show the dirt.' Mr Croucher withheld a whimper of joy. It was the most expensive coffin in the shop.

Lenny slid over the side and lay back in the pink satin padding.

'It feels real fine!' he said. 'Dis is really worth dying for.' He squirmed to make himself more comfortable.

'Now let's try the lid on,' said Mr Croucher.

Carefully he lowered the lid over Lenny's little white face. Shamus raised his voice.

'How's dat feel, Lenny?'

'Very nice,' came the muffled reply.

'Right,' said Shamus addressing Mr Croucher. 'We'll have this one.'

Ruben rubbed his hands with professional pleasure, the dry skin crackling like parchment. Forty years he had sold coffins, but never as quickly as this. His father, the late Hercules Croucher, O.B.E., had founded a fine parlour at Shoreditch. King Edward the Seventh and his ten mistresses were on the throne when the young Ruben was given a black suit for his tenth birthday, that and a scale model replica of the famous Geinsweil Coffin. It awakened in him some deep-rooted instinct; he buried it. Other boys felt girls and played conkers, but little Ruben watched local workmen digging, digging, digging.

'Now sir,' Ruben said, 'if you will step into the office we'll conclude the financial side.'

'You stay there a while,' said Shamus rapping on Lenny's coffin.

In a small room at the back Mr Croucher slid behind an order book and perched on a fountain pen. His black tail coat hung from his shoulders like tired wings. Neatly he took down details in his book. All was silent save the scritch-scratch of his Waverley nib on ruled foolscap.

A great pot of steaming hot Irish stew was heading for the shop at seven miles an hour. It was carried lovingly in the hands of Mrs Ruben Croucher, ex-shot-put champion of Ireland. She walked with a brisk bouncing athletic step, a step forty years younger than her husband's. It had been a most successful marriage. He couldn't do it, and she didn't want to. They had one child. He didn't take after either of them. He did it all the time and walked with a stick. Into the shop bounded the ex-shot-put champion.

'Coooooooeeeee! Are you in there, darling?'

The lid of Lenny's coffin rose up. 'Hello, little darlin',' said Lenny cheerfully.

An Irish stew struck him between the eyes. Mrs Croucher ran screaming from the shop.

'There's your receipt, sir,' said Mr Croucher after carefully counting and recounting thirty-eight carefully forged pound notes.

'We'll take the coffin back on our cart,' said Shamus, standing up.

The culinary arts of the world are varied and a blessing to the sensitive innards of the gourmet, but never in his tour of the globe had Mr Croucher seen a man in a coffin, unconscious and covered in Irish stew.

That night Ruben lay abed cooing through his shrunken gums. A thirty-eight-pound coffin sale. 'Bless us and thank thee, oh Lord, for the merciful benefits thou bestowest on us.' He crossed himself on his home-made prayer, turned slowly on to his good side and fell into a deep peaceful thirty-eight-pound dream. At three o'clock in the morning he died in his sleep. The cost of his funeral came to exactly thirty-eight pounds. His puzzled wife was now in the county jail for passing forged currency. Without her restraining hand her onanistic son now walked with two sticks and a stoop.

Autumn, season of mists and mellow fruitfulness.

'That's a lot of rot,' said Milligan, examining his fingers for frost bite. He scraped the jigsaw of leaves into little funeral pyres. He stooped to light one and warm his hands. The shrill elastic whistle of a robin came clear through the misty morning.

'Awww, shut up, yer idiot!' Milligan was in no mood for nature.

His wages were two weeks overdue and his wife was three.

'I say, Paddy.'

Milligan looked up. Webster was outside the Customs tent beckoning him.

'Me name's not Paddy,' he replied defiantly. He hated Englishmen who called Irishmen 'Paddy'.

'Would you like a cup of tea Paddy?'

'Paddy' Milligan dropped his rake and arrived before it hit the ground.

'It's der first time I had tea with der Customs!'

'Like a dash of whisky?'

'I'll accept dat, sur.'

'Say when.'

'I certainly will not!'

'Found this bottle on a mourner at Dan Doonan's funeral.'

'Oh well, some of dem needs it. Especially the bereaved. I knew a feller so bereaved he could hardly stand.'

In the face of such hospitality, Milligan felt a twinge of conscience, just below the knee. For the last three weeks they had let him through the border without even searching him; in return he had spent his time surreptitiously loosening the earth round Dan Doonan's grave in preparation for the event. All that remained now was for Father Rudden to give the word.

Father Rudden was all ready to give the word but for the unexpected arrival of two ragged-arsed men both smoking the same cigarette and pushing a coffin. Strange. He'd not been notified of a funeral.

'Please, Father,' said Shamus, 'we are poor illiterate farmers, we can't read, write, or post letters. We have pushed the coffin of our grandmother a hundred miles for this burial. We would be grateful if you would officiate.'

Father Rudden was about to refuse when Shamus produced a wad of pound notes. 'Father, we would like to donate dis to the church . . .'

Before Shamus had finished, the priest, never taking his eyes off the money, sprinted backwards to the vestry and returned fully robed with the book open at the service.

One hour later, the customs were examining the beautifully forged passport of the late Mrs Eileen Ford. There followed a solemn burial of two hundred and eighty pounds of T.N.T. Amen.

It was dark when Constable Ah Pong had followed the poacher Rafferty to the vestry of the church. Peering slant-eyed through the window he saw five men donning ragged clothes and whispering. So! Rafferty was the leader of a poaching gang. Disgrace to Ireland! The men were putting pliers and knives down their socks, two were coiling ropes round their

117

waists; their blackened faces made identification impossible. By removing his helmet, remaining still, silent and subservient, Ah Pong could hear the conspirators' conversation.

'It will take five of us to lift it.'

Ah Pong was puzzled – even more difficult, he was puzzled in Chinese.

'What is it poachers caught that took five men to lift?'

He would wait and see. He ran to a tree as the vestry light went out and five shadowy figures came silently from the back door. Goldstein was tying a handkerchief over his face.

'I got to wear it,' he said. 'If anyone sees my nose Rabbi Brody will have me up fer helpin' Catholics.'

Commando-like they tiptoed noisily towards the barbed wire and were swallowed up in the night. His boots round his neck, Ah Pong tiptoed after them.

Chapter Ten

How he'd got on to the wrong side of the border was beyond the comprehension of the idiot Foggerty. He'd been dancing happily alone at the Halloween Ball in the Corn Exchange. Everyone was dressed as a witch or a banshee. Him never having seen either was put to improvising. Foggerty had whitened his face, stuck three chickens' feathers in his hat and painted the sleeve of his overcoat yellow; as an after-thought he stuck little balls of cotton wool on his trousers and boots. He hadn't won a prize but people *had* pointed him out. He was well pleased. He had gone outside to relieve himself when the country gas supply had failed. In the dark he lost his direction and sprayed all over a man called Flood, who gave chase with a stick. For an hour now he had been stumbling oaf-like across unfamiliar territory.

'Helloooooooo!' he wailed. 'Hellooooooooo! I'm getting the hang of this,' he chuckled.

There was no moon; even with it, Foggerty would have been none the brighter. So, collecting evening dew in his hat and calling 'Hello!' he wandered into Northern Ireland, a strange and awesome sight. Even a hungry black panther skulked to the safety of the trees. In his flight Foggerty stumbled over two bodies on the ground. 'Opsss, sorry,' he said, disregarding the rock they threw at him. They waited till he had gone, then continued in their practice of the noble art of nudism, or sunbathing as some say. These two were coming to the end of a long hard day.

On this dark night the sun tan oil glistened on their undulating skins. Locked in a passionate embrace they rolled hither and thither, backwards and forwards through the bushes, drenched with rain, their bodies adhered with passion and clay. They had travelled some thirteen miles like this, not ideal travel but economical.

Watching from the safety of a tree was a man called D. H. Lawrence. He made a hurried note. 'This will make a damned good novel,' he said and hurried off to his Queen's Counsel.

The two sunbathers were now ecstatically groping each other and travelling up a slight incline. For several pubic hours they had fought to extricate all the animal pleasures that were locked in their heaving bodies. Mutual steam was rising from their loins, and the nearest fire brigade ten miles away! Oh, for a bucket of water! Her protruding breasts were pressed flat between his body and hers. He had felt them, he had fondled them; he lifted them, he pressed them, he weighed them, he valued them, he counted them, he massaged them, he stood back from them, he pulled them, he sat on them and picking up a banjo he played them. She clawed at the grass, she clawed at her hair, she clawed the air, she dug her nails into the earth, she dug them into his buttocks. 'Ouch!' he said. Their two mouths were locked in the vacuum of a kiss taut with pulling tongues. Their buttocks tightened and relaxed in never-ending bursts of uncontrollable thrusts of hot coursing gyrations. Inside her, great earthquakes of seminal delight were coursing through her body. He took her nipples in his mouth and drew them into pulsating erection. 'Naughty!' she said. How she loved him, how she worshipped him, this silly old soft-hearted one-eyed negro Lascar off a coaling ship at Belfast. Now the black piston of Africa was helping to cement black-white relationships. He could return to Kenyatta and say the white people love us, let's go back for more. It was over. They lay back gasping.

Next day she took him to meet 'Daddy', the Marshal of the County, Lord Cecil Kasingbroke, v.c., d.s.o. It was the first intimation he had of his daughter's colour blindness. Umboko had run from the stately home, his yellow suit shattered by gun-fire and bull mastiffs, the tribal seat pulverized with buckshot. For weeks he was unable to sit down, even worse, he couldn't stand up. It did, however, prevent white members of the crew having recourse to a certain unsavoury sailor habit.

The heavy metal cutters minced through the barbed wire. O'Brien had cut close to the wooden posts. Father Rudden at his side gave the thumbs up sign. Through the gap, the five men crawled towards the grave of Dan Doonan, rapidly becoming the most travelled corpse in Ireland. Milligan, in the van, cast anxious eyes towards the sentry three hundred yards to their left. A light from the guard hut glinted on the soldier's bayonet. The five men moved to the temporary shelter of an ancient mulberry. Only one hour before two ragged-arsed men had hid in the self-same place. They too had felt for the grave with the loose earth. Soon they were digging up the coffin of Dan Doonan.

'Strange dis T.N.T. doesn't feel so heavy now,' said Shamus.

'No, it doesn't,' said Lenny struggling manfully alone under the weight of the coffin.

Father Rudden led his men forward, his hand too felt for a grave with loose earth.

'Funny, I could have *sworn* it was over there,' said the Milligan as the shovels set to work. Soon the coffin of 'Mrs Eileen Spoleen' with its 200 lb. of T.N.T. was rising.

'Freeze!' said Goldstein.

The party stood, knelt and lay transfixed as a soldier came suspiciously forward. He held his rifle at the ready, he came closer. He stopped, looked cautiously left and right, placed his rifle against a tree. . . . The dirty swine! No wonder the place was starting to smell. They heaved on ropes, sweat was pouring down Milligan's arms.

'Freeze!'

The bloody sentry was coming back; the diggers, gasping, lay flat and still, the ropes cutting their hands.

'Anybody out there?' called the soldier. 'If there's anyone out there say so and I'll fire.' He raised his rifle.

Milligan looked imploringly out of the page.

'For God's sake don't let him shoot, Mister.'

The soldier about-turned and marched away. Milligan grinned.

'God, you got all the power in this book.' He

stroked the stubble on his chin. 'You havin' the power of de author, can I have a request?'

'Yes.'

'Dat dirty soldier that nearly pissed on us, make him do something that will get him into trouble.'

The soldier returned to his post, sloped arms, fired three rounds in the air, dropped his trousers and sang Ave Maria. The Sgt of the Guard came hurrying from his tent.

'Private Worms?' he shouted, 'You're under arrest.'

A powerhouse raspberry was the reply.

'What's going on here?' said Lt Walker, arriving pyjama-clad on the scene.

'I'll show you, sir,' said the sergeant, and inexplicably launched into a series of cartwheels, back somersaults and impressions of Al Jolson in Maltese.

'Both under arrest for being drunk and disorderly. Turn out the guard.'

At the command, the guard assembled and watched him, the Lieutenant, return to his tent with a series of animal noises and great backward leaps on one leg. What would his father Field Marshal Walker, M.C. and Bar, say? Nothing; at this self-same moment he was performing the same feats before his puzzled sovereign at the Passing Out Parade at Sandhurst.

Milligan watched the Lieutenant's antics with a great piano-keyboard smile.

'By Gor, you got the power all right. I wish I was a writer.'

O'Mara put his great shoulders to the rope and pulled the coffin towards the church. 'God, he's heavier since he died, it must suit him.' They all headed for the church leaving Milligan to fill in the grave.

Ah Pong lay lynx-like and silent in a tree of his own choosing. He was about to descend when two shadowy ragged-arsed figures carrying another box headed in the opposite direction. Shamus and Lenny heard a sneeze above them and were hit by a bare-footed falling Chinaman. Running with a coffin-cart they disappeared, firing their pistols in all directions. Ah Pong replied with a burst of whistle-blowing, took a pace backwards and disappeared into an empty grave.

The guard turned out and opened fire. 'The I.R.A.!' went up a cry. A bewildered bugler in underpants blew the lights out and put the whole camp in darkness. Webster leapt from his bed into the po. Barrington fainted in his sleep. Father Rudden and Co. dropped their coffin and ran like hares for cover. Incendiary bullets criss-crossed the night sky, verey lights burst in the darkness. Private Dawson saw a gamboge Chinese face arising from a grave and promptly did in his trousers what cascara takes 24 hours to do.

'Halt, who goes there?' he said, hurriedly tearing up a newspaper.

Quaking with fear the Chinese answered in Pekinese and was immediately fired at in Gaelic. The shot knocked the top off his truncheon. Hysterically he walked up the grave wall and ran chattering into the night. 'Sod that for a lark,' he said. He really was getting a grip on the language.

It was 4.32. The firing had died away. There was an uneasy silence. The soldiers strained their ears. Then from the distance came the unmistakable sound of an unidentified noise. 'Helloooooooo!' it went. The voice was strange to them, but not to Foggerty. The corporal made a signal to his men.

'This might be a trick, hold yer fire till I give three short blasts on me whistle.'

'Hellooooo!' It was coming closer. Running. Ah Pong tripped over Milligan's shovel. Heroically he blew three blasts on his whistle, and Foggerty received the full ballistic weight of B Coy's fire power.

The moon came out, its silver beams streaming through the bullet holes in Foggerty's trousers and hat. Life is a matter of majorities, either you have one or you haven't. Right now Foggerty was outvoted.

The dawn came up like thunder out of China across the bay. It didn't do that in Ulster. Shivering and swearing, Lenny and Shamus scraped the hoar frost from their faces and pushed Dan Doonan's coffin into the bushes.

'We can't hang around here, Lenny, they'll be looking for us on both sides now. What bloody bad luck. We'll leave this T.N.T. there till the hooha dies down.'

Lenny nodded woefully as he arranged the bracken on top of the coffin. Sad yes, this little lot was supposed to blow up that police station at Durragh. The sound of a bugle being bugled broke the morning silence. Lenny hid behind Shamus.

'Is that the Military?' he said.

'I don't know, it cummed from over there.'

The two men climbed to the lip of a hill and peered cautiously over. A fine sight met their eyes; gleaming white in the morning sun were the tents of that knobbly-kneed society, the Scouts.

It was the Ulster Annual Jamboree. For weeks past, hundreds of spotty-faced herberts, with yodelling voices and chin fuzz, had tied three million knots, started ten thousand twig fires, and completed six hundred leaf shelters; perfect training for round about 3,000 BC but bloody useless in the twentieth century. Where were their geiger counters? Their strontium detectors? Their books on how to bury ten million incinerated children? Be prepared? Ha! Ha!

Shamus could just read the sign, 'Scout Store. Re-kitting Section.' Scouts of all sizes were lining up for a fine breakfast of burnt eggs and carbonized toast when two ragged-arsed men slipped unnoticed under the flaps of a marquee. Chief Scoutmaster Theobald Dring looked on approvingly. What a fine bunch of lads. He felt fine too. He examined himself. He was fine. He looked fine. Fifty-seven fine years old, tall, erect, clear skinned, fine broad shoulders, slender hips; fine muscular arms, short bow legs. He had overcome this latter handicap by stuffing newspapers down the inside of his hose, and thus managed to build up the calves sufficiently to match the extensive outward curve of the leg. It did however give him the unfortunate appearance of a man with 29-inch calves, and a man with 13-inch thighs can't do that sort of thing.

He yawned and rose from his sapling and sheep-shank bed. Strange, he thought as he searched for his shaving kit, it was there last night.

Two cleanly shaved scouts in new but ill-fitting uniforms enjoyed the pleasure of an alfresco breakfast without payment.

'Oh-ho,' said Lenny, 'dis is a stroke of luck, no one but Baden-Powell would tink of lookin' for us here.'

Shamus nodded in agreement, his mouth moving relentlessly on a slice of dead pig recumbent on a sea of porridge.

'Pardon me, sir,' said a small scout sitting opposite, his face held together with pimples, 'what troop are you from?'

'The 3rd Puckoon Rangers,' said Shamus, licking his lips, plate, knife, fork, spoon, fingers and thumbs.

Twelve miles north of Puckoon, set in rolling acres, rose the delicate Georgian facades of Brent Lodge, built in an age when craftsmen loved the excitement of creation, be it only brick upon brick. Now it lay open to its greatest enemy, the twentieth century. The proportions were for all to see, uncrowded, with an eternal grace culled from Ancient Greece. Soane had built it for the Dukes of Munster, who, falling short of money and an heir, willed it to the people of Ulster in perpetuity. In the hands of the local Council, it had been reduced to 'Units of Housing'. Aged gentlefolk, retired Colonels and widowed matrons now lived out their lives in the grim indifference of local government. The tall, beautiful, curved glass windows looked out on once toparied hedges, now long untrimmed; lily ponds and choked fountains graced the lawns the local council had recently officially 'cut', with a bread knife it would appear. There it now stood, a masterpiece of yesterday, ignored by the bureaucratic barbarism of today. Soon, the Chairman of the Council Planning Committee would gather strength from statistics, revenue, and a chorus of 'Ayes' from his sycophantic minions, and order it to be 'pulled down'. To the press he would issue a well-thumbed paper ' – too expensive to maintain, etc., etc., etc., make way for etc., etc., etc., sentimentalism must not stop progress etc., etc., etc.' Bureaucracy was the counterpart of cancer, it grew bigger and destroyed everything except itself.

Before this monster stood Brent Lodge. The wind was blowing flakes of paint from its lintels and pediments. Occasionally a refined old face would part the heavy, long, faded velveteen curtains, then slowly recede into the oblivion of the great house. The two tall, double-fronted, mahogany wood doors with their unpolished brass handles were reached by twelve gently ascending marble steps, flanked by Venetian balustrades; on top, supported by two slender columns, was a portico surmounted by a Greek frieze. On the doorstep stood a half-pint bottle of grade 2 milk. A thick veiny but refined hand withdrew it into the hall.

The youngest member of this ageing community was ex-variety artiste, Patrick L. Balls. Fifty-nine now, he spent out his remaining years pulling a rope lift and bottling fruit. He had once whistled Ave Maria for Queen Victoria. She wasn't present at the time, but nevertheless that's who he was whistling it for.

Today would be very busy. No whistling for him. Today was the Concert. Once a year the scouts came and 'did a concert of talking'. Tonight they would perform in the Hydro Hall a drastically cut version of 'The Immortal Bard', *Julius Caesar*.

The indoor plunge bath in the Hydro was boarded over, and the great French windows were folded back to make way for the temporary stage that backed on to the garden. Behind this, jacked up on its back axle was the 1909 de Dion, whose yellow wheels drove the power for the footlights. Slowly now, the hall was filling with the spectre-like audience. The sisters, Agnes and Millicent Grope, walked mincingly down the aisle on Minny Mouse legs, fox furs around their long, thin white necks.

'It's *Julius Caesar* again then,' said Agnes, taking her seat.

'It was *Julius Caesar* last year, Agnes.'

'Oh? I suppose this is an encore,' smiled Agnes, opening her programme. Preparing themselves in the orchestra pit were the Patrick Furg 'Refined' Trio. A doddering trinity of febrile musicians, led by a bent, thin violinist. The piano keyboard lay staring up at Mrs Auraulum Murphy, a short, tubby, middle-aged lady with amber beads and a dropped womb. She clipped her music to the stand with clothes pegs, a present from a musical laundry man. Behind her, supporting herself on a 'cello was Madame Elsie Mooney, who ran her resin listlessly across the hairs of her bow; her long stringy neck and pendulous jowls gave her the appearance of a plucked turkey. She was dressed carefully in a sea of brown Majorca lace; brittle white hair escaped in all directions from its prison of hairpins; she turned her lizard-like gaze at the stage. A small, hastily made-up, roseate face appeared from the wings. 'Psssstt, ready in two minutes,' it said and disappeared. Madame Mooney prodded Patrick's stern with her bow.

'Don't do that Madame Mooney!' he said. 'It pleasures me not any more.'

'They'll be ready in two minutes, Patrick.'

'Oh.' Patrick checked his music. 'Did you hear that, Miss Murphy?'

She nodded her head.

'A tuning A please.' He plucked the sagging strings to order, then in a jocular mood, drew the bow fiercely across the bridge with all the fire of decay. 'How's *that*!' he said.

'Out!' shouted an old cricket fan in the audience.

Miss Murphy tittered at him. He had proposed to her thirty-seven times in ten years and been refused. Last week she had proposed to him, and he was now considering it.

Both conversation and the house lights went down; a few exhibition coughers voiced their bronchial ego; the silence that followed was shattered by two loud thumps of Patrick Furg's boots, and the refined trio launched shakily into several bars of obscure music. 'Good God!' said a music lover finally, 'It's – it's William Tell.'

Slowly the front curtain rose rapidly, stuck and crashed down again. It rose rapidly. Got stuck and stayed stuck rapidly. It revealed a forest of anonymous legs. Two embarrassed Scoutmasters with overcoats hastily donned over togas, shuffled on the stage. With sticks and whispered orders, the obstinate curtain was raised. Fronting four and twenty Roman spearsmen were three steps covered in army blankets; flanking this stood two canvas and lath Doric columns painted on brown paper. The programme note: Rome. The steps of the Imperial Palace. How the old place had changed. Standing on this noble pile, the figure of an eight-year-old Cassius was speaking; proud and erect he stood in his white bed-sheet and cardboard laurel leaves, in his pocket a complete set of great footballer cigarette cards. To the refined ear, trained for euphony, Shakespeare rings most comforting; to a Roman spearsman named Shamus Ford it brought a mental remark, 'What the hell's this all about?' To his left Lenny was thinking that he didn't look too bad as a Roman soldier. Cassius raised his hands to silence the mob. The great curtain crashed to the stage. This time the Patrick Furg trio were ready.

'Emergency One,' said Patrick to his trio. Off they went, reducing in three minutes a reputation Rossini had taken one hundred years to establish. After further sticks, pushes and shouts the curtain rose again. The same scene plus, at no additional cost, happily smoking Centurion. Shamus snatched the cigarette from Lenny's mouth.

From back stage there was a metallic clang. . . . The silencer had fallen from the generator car and the ensuing noise of the open exhaust forced the young actors to shout, causing one Roman's nose to bleed. A change of wind was now blowing smoke from the long carbonized car engine, up through the cracks in the stage; the cast were now reduced to shouting *and* coughing. 'Beware the Ides of March,' said the soothsayer, losing his beard in a fit of coughing. The smoke obscured the players who all moved forward to the footlights. Unaffected, the Furg trio were playing the Hall of the Mountain Kings, with a difference; the rising warmth of the thermal waters below them was gradually lowering the pitch of their instruments; gradually the Hall of the Mountain Kings slid chromatically from C Major down to B Flat Minor.

'Crazy, man,' whispered Patrick.

The smoke had caused a disturbed deaf member of the audience to phone the fire brigade. 'Come quick, Brent Lodge is in flames, thousands are trapped!' was the simple message.

In the front row was guest of honour, Inspector Tomelty. For ten minutes he had been wrestling with the face of a certain Roman soldier. Suddenly he clicked his fingers. 'Shamus Ford! Excuse me,' he said, pushing along a row of creaking arthritic legs. Soon two Black Marias thundered in the night, during which time the audience were treated to the spectacle of six men in brass helmets dashing on a smoke-filled stage with hoses; they immediately set about the floor with hatchets and with the first stroke three toes came off. Smoke now obscured the cast from the audience. Groping forward, a fat Julius Caesar tripped and fell on to the piano; eighteen stone of Julian flesh was all it needed to send the instrument crashing through the floor beneath; with a splintering groan the Patrick

Furg Trio, all playing valiantly, slid majestically into the warm waters of the hydro pool below. A chain reaction followed as the temporary floor broke into sections, everywhere were floating rafts bearing the trapped, shouting, aged audience. The De Dion had fallen off its blocks and ripped the backcloth away, revealing twenty scouts in various stages of undress. Hoses were starting to douse the last remaining actors. Police whistles announced new arrivals. Shouts of help came from the marooned audience.

'Let's beat it,' said Shamus pulling Lenny with him.

They reached the first floor with the police at their heels. The lift! A gift from above! Slamming the gates, Shamus gave the ancient rope the pull of its rotting life. It snapped. The ancient lift hurtled down the shaft, hit the rubber buffers in the basement and hurtled up again. It hovered at the third floor 'twixt momentum and gravity, *just* long enough for an unsuspecting chambermaid to step in and hurtle down again.

'Have we got the electric on?' she smiled at the terrified occupants.

Patrick Balls not wanting to spend his remaining years yo-yoing in a lift, grabbed at the end of the frayed rope as it came within reach and was left hanging as the lift hurtled down again. Rocketing up, Shamus and Lenny judged the pause and leaped out at the second floor.

Cries of 'Send help!' came from the plummeting gentlefolk. Colonel Carrington-Thurk R.A., Retd., awoke from his slumbers, heard the cacophony, and leapt from his bed; sabre in hand he opened the door and fell over a fire hose.

'Take that, you Indian swine!' he yelled, slicing through the pulsating canvas; a deluge of water from the hose jack-knifed him back into the dumb waiter which descended at speed to the kitchen.

On the end of the ruptured hose, Fireman Mortimer Wreggs suddenly held a lifeless bronze nozzle in his hand. 'Bugger!' he said, 'Oh bugger, bugger, bugger!' and lay face down on the floor threshing his legs in temperamental spasms. This emotional outburst was of deep Freudian significance; had not Adler, Freud and Jung all agreed that the seeds of hereditary ambition are passed on through successive generations until fulfilment? So was it with young Fireman Wreggs. His great-great-grandfather had *almost* extinguished the greatest and most expensive fire in the history of Ireland, but alas, in the best traditions of British services had arrived too late!

That fearful conflagration was a mighty story in the annals of the family Wreggs. The disintegration of the Austro-Hungarian Empire hit many people, especially those who had disintegrated with it. The Count Nuker-Frit-Kraphauser was one such notable. In the hiatus that followed the assassination of the Archduke Ferdinand, and the collapse of the Empire, he had fled his native Hungary in the jade of a revolutionary night with nothing save a small suitcase with three million pounds and some silly old crown jewels, but this fortune meant nothing; his greatest loss was having to leave the great and majestic family Easence. The greatest toilet in the western world and the only consecrated one in the Holy Roman Empire.

The Count Fritz Von Krappenhauser had fled to

Northern Ireland, bought Callarry Castle, ten thousand acres, and a small packet of figs. For years he brooded over the loss of the ancestral abort. Finally worn out by indifferent, and severe wood-seated Victorian commodes, he decided to build a replica of the family's lost masterpiece here in the heart of Ulster's rolling countryside. He employed the greatest baroque and Rococo architects and craftsmen of the day, and every day after; seven years of intense labour, and there it now stood, a great octagonal Easence. No ordinary palace was this; from the early stone Easence of Bodiam Castle to the low silent suite at the Dorchester is a long strain, but nothing equalled this, its gold leaf and lapis lazuli settings gleaming in the morning sun, on the eight-sided walls great ikons of straining ancestors, a warning to the unfit. Through a Moorish arch of latticed stone, one entered the 'Throne Room'; above it, in Gothic capitals the family motto, 'Abort in Luxus'. From the centre rose a delicate gilded metal and pink alabaster commode. Six steps cut in black Cararra marble engraved with royal mottoes led up to the mighty Easence; it was a riot of carefully engraved figurines in the voluptuous Alexandrian style, depicting the history of the family with myriad complex designs and sectionalized stomachs in various stages of compression. The seat was covered in heavy wine damask velvet, the family coat of arms sewn petit-point around the rim in fine gold thread. Inside the pan were low relief sculptures of the family enemies, staring white-faced in expectation. Towering at the four corners, holding a silk tasselled replica of the Bernini canopy, were four royal beasts, their snarling jaws containing ashtrays and matches. Bolted to the throne were ivory straining bars carved with monkeys and cunningly set at convenient angles; around the base ran a small bubbling perfumed brook whose water welled from an ice-cool underground stream. Gushes of warm air passed up the trouser legs of the sitter, the pressure controlled by a gilt handle. By pedalling hard with two foot-levers the whole throne could be raised ten feet to allow the sitter a long drop; and even greater delight, the whole Easence was mounted on ball-bearings. A control valve shaped like the crown of Hungary would release steam power that would revolve the commode. There had been a time when the Count had aborted revolving at sixty miles an hour and been given a medal by the Pope.

White leather straps enabled him to secure himself firmly during the body-shaking horrors of constipation. Close at hand were three burnished hunting horns of varying lengths. Each one had a deep significant meaning. The small one when blown told the waiting household all was well, and the morning mission accomplished. The middle one of silver and brass was blown to signify that there might be a delay. The third one, a great Tibetan Hill Horn, was blown in dire emergency; it meant a failure and waiting retainers would rush to the relief of the Count, with trays of steaming fresh enemas ready to be plunged into action on their mission of mercy and relief. With the coming of the jet age the noble Count had added to the abort throne an ejector mechanism. Should there ever be need he could, whilst still in throes, pull a lever and be shot three hundred feet up to float gently down on a parachute. The stained glass windows when open looked out on to 500 acres of the finest grouse shooting moor in Ulster. He had once invited Winston Churchill to come and shoot from the sitting position. In reply Churchill sent a brief note, 'Sorry, I have business elsewhere that day.' From his commode, the Count could select any one of a number of fine fowling pieces and bring down his dinner. Alas, this caused his undoing. The boxes of 12-bore cartridges, though bought at the best shops in London, had sprung a powder leak. Carelessly flicking an early morning cigar, the hot ash had perforated the wad of a cartridge.

But to the day of the calamitous fire. It had been a fine morning that day in 1873. The Count had just received his early morning enema of soap suds and spice at body heat; crying 'Nitchevo!' he leapt from his couch. Colonic irrigation and enemas had made his exile one internal holiday. Clutching a month-old copy of *Der Tag*, and contracting his abdomen, he trod majestically towards his famed Imperial outdoor abort bar. A few moments later the waiting retainers heard a shattering roar and were deluged, among other things, with rubble.

'Himmel? Hermann? What did you put in the last enema?' queried the family doctor of the retainers.

Flames and debris showered the grounds and there, floating down on the parachute, came the Count. 'People will look to me when I die,' he had once said. His wish had come true.

In that fire had perished Fireman Wreggs. Now his

great-grandson lay there crying on the floor of Brent Lodge House. The pandemonium had snowballed and perfectly good friends were hitting each other.

'*There is no fire!*' a very angry Scoutmaster was saying, his paper columns flattened with water. 'There is no fire!' he repeated as three firemen poured eighty gallons a minute over him. 'You're ruining our costumes!' he shouted. They silenced him by increased water pressure, at a hundred gallons a minute he was sluiced backwards into a choked lily pond.

'Three troop to the rescue!' he shouted through his umbrella of water lilies.

Solitary and floating alone in her row 'D8' chair, its planks awash, was stone-deaf Miss Penelope Dingley-Smythe, her hearing aid turned to zero. She snored oblivious of the hydro waters that lapped at the soles of her little Victorian high-button boots. The Brigade were being severely hampered by two things, a lack of water, and a lack of fire. Of the thirteen hoses only six were at full pressure. Frantically lighting fires as he went, Fire Chief Muldoon discovered a rusty verdigris board covered in turncocks. 'Hallelujah!' he exalted as he turned the lot on. There was a rumbling sound under the earth. Long forgotten fountains lived again, eroded pipes burst in all directions, streams of water shot from under many an unsuspecting victim. Thirty great jets hurled a screaming scoutmaster twenty feet in the air, ripping his boots and socks from his feet. Once gentle bidets suddenly gushed up unsuspecting old females, giving a mixed feeling of fear and joy. The delightful Juno-esque fountain Naiad, her innards clogged this many a year, suddenly burst. Old Admiral Munroe under his shower was flattened by the increase in water power. The ancient brass geyser was trying to consume the new rate of intake and remain intact; with steam everywhere, it started to boil and fall apart. As the Admiral took to his heels, it exploded and hurled him naked into the corridor right on to the teatray outside the door; seated on it like an aged Puck, he slid powerless down the steps shouting 'Foreeeeeee!' Tightly holding the edge of his slender craft it hurtled down the wet stairs into the hall, and finally shot out the front doors on to the lawn at the feet of Mrs Grimblenack. 'Madame!' roared the quick-witted Admiral, 'Get out of my bathroom!' But she would have none of his finesse. 'If you don't go to my bedroom at once I'll scream!' she said. He fled into the countryside and later was found dead from indecent exposure.

Chapter Eleven

Repulsed by gunfire, his hat full of bullet holes, Foggerty retreated deeper and deeper into Ulster. In the dark he had seen two men running, swearing and carrying a coffin on their heads. 'Hello fellas,' he had said, 'it's me, Foggerty.' In reply a fist had cudgeoned on his forehead. It was daylight when he regained consciousness. 'I musta' been tired!' he yawned. It was two days since he had last eaten. He was hungry. I could eat a horse, he thought. He walked several paces, when a horse strayed across his path. 'Mmmm, it's too big to eat,' he thought. 'I know, I'll ride it till it gets slimmer.' The animal bolted with him.

It took him a-galloping and screaming into the grounds of Brent Lodge, at the very moment when a Roman soldier dashed from the main entrance pursued hotly by the police. In one rough move the son of Rome took Foggerty's ankle, flung him from the horse, bounded on to the animal and galloped like the wind from the grounds, followed by the police. Stunned and mudspattered, Foggerty lay white and still on the ground.

But help was coming a' running. Down the steps came a black chiffon-swathed harpy-like female; it was Madame Elaine Grinns, spiritualist, mystique, laundress and amateur necrophile. Twenty years she had forecast the return of her dead, sex-mad husband Nugent Grinns on the back of a wild stallion; agreed, the horse had turned out to be an old farm hack, but then he always was a modest man. Now there he lay, white faced and grinning, the feathers of a chieftain in his crown. Gently she raised his head. 'Nugent, you have returned!'

'Hello, little darlin,' said Foggerty, grateful for any attention.

Slowly she led him up the great steps into the smoking interior of the laundry room. 'You must rest,' she said, 'You have been dead a long time.'

'Oh?' said Mr Foggerty. 'Dead, eh? Well I suppose it happens to der best of us. What's for lunch?'

'Food later, dear,' she said starting to remove his clothes.

'Here, here, here,' said the startled Foggerty, 'I'm not eatin' naked.'

'Nugent dear, you know very well I *must* rub you with oil and spices, as was our custom,' she reminded him.

'But I'm hungry,' he insisted, holding on to his trousers.

'Come, come, dear,' she said rolling up her sleeves, 'I don't want to have to kill you again, you know how unpleasant it was last time.'

'Eh?' said Foggerty.

The Customs camp and its attendant soldiers were returning to normal after the night's ructions. 'They must have been I.R.A. I suppose, Sergeant?' said Lt Walker.

'Oh yes sur,' was the confident reply. 'No one else fires so many rounds and misses.'

A clatter of hooves. What appeared to be a Roman soldier galloped up to the sentry. 'Halt!' he called.

'Have you seen a circus go this way?' said Shamus.

'Er, no.'

'Say sir when you speak to Julius Caesar!' rapped Shamus.

'Sir!'

The Roman lashed his mount and galloped over the frontier towards the back of the church.

'Who the blazes was that?' said Lt Walker doubling across.

'Julius Caesar,' said the sentry, and wondered why he was demoted on the spot.

The sky was stone black with the promise of snow. The glass was falling. The Atlantic tossed its cold white curls into the wind. Sitting by an oil stove in the vestry, Mr Pills the verger polished the altar silver and sang. 'La de de de, de da de de,' he hummed softly stopping occasionally to blow his cold wet nose. The vestry was draughty and large and the only thing warm was the stove itself. Occasionally he stopped to run one hand over the top vents, catching the streams of warm air between his fingers. This weather was terrible on his feet, the circulation seemed only to go as far as his insteps. From the welts of his boots he left a trail of yellow powder. An old Australian lady called Miss Blewitt had told him of the trick when he was a seaman on board the old P. & O. liner the *Kaiser Hind*. 'Put plenty of sulphur in your socks and you'll never suffer from tuberculosis.' And true as true, touch wood, for forty-eight years since he put sulphur in his socks, he had never had the disease; he hadn't had it before mark you, but he definitely hadn't had it since.

Old remedies were sometimes the best. Had not the leeks sewn in the waist band of his long underwear staved off leprosy? And where would he be without the dried onion skins in a bag around his neck? Dead from malaria for sure! One thing he hadn't got a cure for was bad circulation, strange that, the one thing he did suffer from, no one had a cure for. He had invoked the saints and had burned many candles asking for 'Help for me poor cold feet'. The saints had ignored him – he did however notice that the candles had a better effect when they were held under his feet. 'La la la de de de,' he went. He watched the satisfying glint of old silver as it shone through the plate powder.

From the corner of the room came the conspiratorial whisper of Father Rudden talking rapidly to the Milligan. Father placed one hand on Milligan's shoulder. 'We'll re-bury him tonight in Holy Catholic Ireland,' said the priest, his voice full of pride and achievement.

'You realize that we've only got two more dear souls to bring back and we've won,' he waved his hands aloft like battle flags. 'People will point to you in the street.'

'Dey do dat already,' said Milligan disgruntedly.

'Ahh! But this will be different, you'll be a hero! There he goes, they'll say, or, here he comes, according to the direction you're travelling. On top of that, if the Pope gets to hear of it, you could be made a Papal Knight.'

'Me, a Papal Knight?' Milligan screwed his eyes

up to get a better vision of himself walking up the steps of the Vatican.

'How are yer, Milligan me boy?' the Pope would say.

'I'm fine, yer honour,' the Milligan would reply.

'My, my, my, Milligan, you done a fine job o' work diggin' up them stiffs and bringin' 'em back to consecrated ground.'

Milligan would smile, 'Well yer honour, anything fer the old Church.'

Then the trumpets would blare out Danny Boy by Cellini and the Pope would give him a certificate, two pounds, and a bottle of holy water. 'Arise, Sir Papal Knight The Milligan.'

'All right Fadder,' said Milligan, 'I'll do it.'

'And remember, Milligan,' the priest said, a look of profound wisdom on his face, 'there's an old Irish saying – ' he paused, his eyes closed as though searching his soul. Milligan stood quietly by.

The priest opened his eyes, 'I can't quite remember it at the moment,' he concluded.

Outside the gardener's hut Milligan paused to light his pipe; a hairy arm reached out from the shed and laced around his throat dragging him back.

'This is a gun in yer back,' hissed a hoarse voice.

'All right,' gasped Milligan, 'as long as you don't shoot I can stand it.'

The arm uncurled. He turned to see Shamus Ford.

'Look lively,' said the gunman, 'take yer clothes off, hurry.'

The pistol's blue mouth was directed at Milligan's

heart. Slowly Milligan removed his trousers, not without a feeling of apprehension.

'Dere's a limit to what I'll do,' he warned the gunman.

Milligan wondered if this strange metal-clad figure was one of them homosexual murderers that were so popular in better educated countries. Naked, save for his socks, Milligan was told to stand in the corner of the hut with his hands above his head.

'Now,' said the voice, 'you'll stay facing that way.'

The door closed behind him. The outside bolt went home. He heard the gunman's horse gallop away. Snow was starting to fall. It was cold. Milligan lit the stove and started to shout for help. Next to the stove the coffin started to singe.

Mr Moris Prells walked with mathematical precision up the church drive. He had the white blotting-paper complexion of a man who worked under cover and slept with the windows closed. In his wallet, Mr Prells carried ten neat calling cards wrapped in tissue paper. They were printed: *Mr Julian S. Prells, County Quantitive Surveyor. Department of Weights, Measures and Statistics.*

Mr Prells calculated that at that very moment his age was forty-seven years, three months, two days, ten hours and forty minutes. His weight with the grey suit was one hundred and sixty-eight pounds, three ounces. Life was a precise affair. One was better equipped to face it with facts and figures at one's disposal. It gave one a sense of certainty in an uncertain world. At this very moment, if anyone were to ask him the precise weight of the sewerage discharged by

Puckoon he could answer down to the fine ounce. At parties he often told people without being asked. One must have facts and figures. Each and every one of us is a fact and a figure. His little meek wife, walking on an invisible chain at his side, she was a fact and figure. In fact, at eighteen she had been a very good figure. From his attic room he was able to watch her undress. Even from that distance he was able to jot down 36, 20, 36. That was twenty-three years and five months ago; last week he had bought her a pair of corsets 43, 29, 42, in memory of those happy 36, 20, 36 days.

Together they were strolling up the church drive to evening devotions. He gauged his stride as two feet nine inches, and each foot would weigh roughly a pound. Oh yes, these little statistical walks with his wife gave him much information. One statistic he wasn't aware of. The ever-widening gap between him and her. And the ever-narrowing one between her and the coalman. Suddenly his calculations were interrupted.

'Pssttttttttttttttt!' Mr Prells stopped. 'Pssssssttttttttt!' There it was again, well not exactly again. This was a *second* Psssttt but sounded exactly the same as the first. 'Pssttttttttttt!' It appeared to be coming from inside the gardener's shed. There must be someone in residence. Smoke was coming from the chimney. Mr Prells leaned towards the door and spoke.

'Who's in there going "Psssttt"?' he inquired.

'Me name's Milligan. Dan Milligan.'

'I'm very pleased to meet you,' said Prells through the keyhole, and raising his hat. 'My name is Prells

146

and this is my wife Hetty.' So saying he slid one of his cards under the door.

'Please unbolt the door, it's a matter of life and death.' Deftly Mr Prells withdrew the bolt, the door opened slowly, and there stood Milligan, the Roman Soldier.

Before he could explain, there was a crunch of Ulster Police boots on gravel. 'That's the feller!' shouted the Sergeant. In a moment, Milligan went under to a sea of flailing truncheons and snapping handcuffs. 'Thang!' went the truncheons on Milligan's helmet. 'Thang! Thang!' Mr Prells assessed that each truncheon would weigh three pounds, there were five of them, they were descending on Milligan's head at the rate of one blow every three seconds, therefore, five by three gave a total weight of fifteen pounds per combined hit, fifteen pounds every three seconds, therefore in one hour's hitting the man in the Roman helmet would receive $15 \times 3 = 45$ lbs in weight. A good weight.

'Helppppp! Stop!' screamed Milligan, 'Stopppppp! I surrender!'

'Not till we've finished you don't,' came the gleeful reply.

'Stop, I got something important to tell you,' said the Milligan. The relentless thudding stopped. 'Well, what is it?' asked the Sergeant. 'You're a lot of Protestant Bastards, that's what!' said Milligan, immediately going into the foetal position. 'Thang!' went the truncheons with renewed vigour. 'Thang – Thang Thang!'

Through the blue serge legs, Milligan saw a small

148

tent of blue that the prisoner called the sky. He took it. Up the road he ran, his left wrist handcuffed to his right ankle. Rocks bounced off his skull. The police were gaining, proof positive that five pairs of legs are faster than one. 'Help, me legs are outnumbered!' he shouted, the light of despair coming into his eyes.

'SQUORROX!' he yelled.

Francois D'Fruites, tall, thin, passionate, mustachioed croupier at the Monte Carlo tables, was momentarily puzzled; he had not previously noticed this unshaven man in the exquisite evening clothes. Nevertheless there he was now. The man appeared breathless, repeatedly looking over his shoulder and occasionally feeling his legs. The man suddenly looked at his own garb in great surprise, then his face broke into a broad relieved grin. A highly suspicious manager had inquired of him, 'Can I be of help, m'sieur?' and was answered with, 'Speak English, you ignorant swine.'

'Pardon?' said the manager, lapsing into English. 'May I see your membership card?'

'Sure,' said the Milligan, producing a million-franc note. 'Dere it is me old froggie lad, and dere's more where dat came from,' he said, waving a fistful in his face.

The manager swayed slightly. 'Merci,' he was heard to say very feebly.

A creature in red velvet, white skin and raven hair, reeking of all the latest anti-underarm odours, saw the money and was suddenly drawn towards this fascinating stranger.

'Good evening, you naughty man,' she said,

affectionately stroking his currency, and smiled at him from a forty-two inch bosom.

Milligan knew that the more a woman's bust protrudes the more her mind recedes.

'Hello, little darlin',' he said from the waist down. 'Vous le vous promenade avec moi?' he said from his little store of 1914 French. 'Kaiser Bill fini,' he informed her.

'Meet me at zis address,' she said, slipping him a well-thumbed picture of a bedroom. 'We will 'ave a good time, not to mention Bazonka.'

'Bazonka?' he queried.

'I told you not to mention that!' she said.

He slipped his arm around her waist, even as he did five Ulster police burst through the main Casino door. 'There's the bastard!' shouted the leading one. 'Thang!' went the first truncheon on Milligan's skull.

'It sounds like him, lads,' said the Sergeant.

'Thankety-thang-thang!' went the truncheons.

'What's going on here?' said Father Rudden issuing from the vestry, his face covered in shaving soap. 'What are you doing in me churchyard?' he roared, pulling off a layer of policemen.

'This man is a member of the I.R.A., sir,' they said pointing at the Milligan.

'Nonsense, this man is my gardener.'

'Then your gardener is a member of the I.R.A.,' they said dragging Milligan away.

'Stop!' said the priest. 'Gentlemen,' he said in tones most contrite, but continuing to shave, 'if you'll step into the vestry, I will admit the entire plot to capture the Queen.'

The Sergeant dropped his truncheon with shock. This was a turn-up for the book.

'Very well,' said the Sergeant, 'first I'll want a signed confession.'

The priest stood to one side, he was not numerically equipped to stand more. 'In here,' he said.

One by one the police filed into the vestry. The door slammed behind.

'Run for the polis and the militia!' they heard him shout to Milligan.

The trapped men were hammering on the inside of the door and nails started to fly like confetti. The priest was shaving as fast as he could. In the gardener's hut, the wood of the coffin was starting to smoulder, and somewhere a drunk called Hermonogies K. Thuckrutes lay face down in a gutter singing.

The wind blew bitter cold. Twenty-four hours since the panther escaped. Mr Wretch and Gulio Caesar looked miserably at each other. The creature must have crossed the border. The cage pulled up at the Customs post, wearily Gulio let himself to the ground and approached a smarting sentry. 'Just let him tell me his name is Julius Caesar,' he thought.

'Pardona me,' said the little Italian, 'mya name is Gulio Caesar – ' The next moment he was on his back, the soldier jumping up and down on his stomach, a bayonet at his nose. 'And I'm Brutus!' yelled the gleeful soldier. He was eventually restrained by Barrington.

'What do you want?' he asked the unfortunate Gulio.

'We wanta to crossa da border.'

'Then I must examine the cage for contraband.' He entered the cage up three steps. The horse gave a little lurch. The cage door slammed, now, it was one of those tricky locks. . . .

With Ah Pong on the pillion, Sergeant MacGillikudie cycled to investigate the Chinaman's report of 'mass poachings'. Snow was falling and the little yellow man's gold teeth were chattering with eighteen carat gold. Turning a corner they came upon a hopping Roman, ankle handcuffed to wrist, who for the last mile had been desperately trying to mount a bike and would have been well advised to leave it alone.

'Milligan!' shouted MacGillikudie. 'What in God's name are you doing?'

Without warning his pillion passenger, the Sergeant dismounted, his boot contacting Ah Pong's gold teeth and thus devaluing the Chinaman's head by thirty Hong Kong dollars.

Standing up bent double, Milligan gabbled out the story.

'Quick, on the cross bar,' said MacGillikudie.

Downhill rode the avenging trio, the wind howling through the gap in Ah Pong's teeth. Faster and faster revolved the Sergeant's legs, his mind occupied with thoughts of massive arrests and promotion.

'Ah Pong,' said Sergeant MacGillikudie, 'I am exceeding the speed limit, I want you to *book me.*'

'I do,' said the Chinese.

'Good, now I arrest you as you are going the same speed!' The Law was the law.

For an hour they hammered and banged on the lock of the cage. It was starting to snow.

'Someone go and get an acetylene cutter,' said Barrington gripping the bars.

'Mama mia, no no,' said Gulio, 'data would ruin da lock!'

'There's a locksmith in Puckoon,' said Mr Wretch, 'a retired burglar, he wants to get his hand in again.'

'Anything,' said Barrington, 'but get me out of this frightful cage.'

Mr Wretch turned the pony towards Puckoon.

They were puzzled farmworkers who watched the cage with its attendant shouting-skipping-alongside children. It had got to the poking him with sticks stage.

'Get away, dem you!' shouted Barrington.

'What hav yez done rong mister?'

'Was it a murder?'

'Have you got a diz-ease?'

A pebble hit Barrington on his aristocratic ear. 'Stop that!' he fumed. Another pebble bounced off his neck. 'And stop that as well!' This only invoked a shower of stones, orange peels, toffee papers, spits, sherbet sticks, and incessant tauntings. In a frenzy, under a non-stop barrage of ridicule and missiles, Barrington retaliated with a trick usually performed by enraged male chimpanzees in zoos. Soon the pony outstripped the penny-rich children, leaving them in their laughter-diced air. In the cage Barrington nursed a stinging member that some little dead eye dick had hit with a nettle.

At a steady trot Gulio Caesar headed for Puckoon.

God in heaven, what was this? Mr Wretch stood up and went vest-white.

'L-l-look!' He pointed an obstetrical finger. There coming down the hill, were three terrified men on a bike, pursued by – was it? – the panther! Gulio tried to rein, but the pony had seen it, about turned, whinnied and bolted towards the border. The three men on the bike shot past the cart, screaming and saying the rosary; the panther changed its stride, leaped on to the cage, and started slashing down at the cowering Barrington.

Hypodermic at the ready, Mr Wretch sat rooted with fear.

'Stick eet in-a his bum!' shouted Gulio over the noise.

Mr Wretch stood up, stumbled, and fell needle first into Gulio's thigh; he gave one loud shriek then fell into a deep smiling-faced Neapolitan sleep.

Haring past them went a lorry with the Republic militia, the bulb horn clearing the way. At the wheel sat Sergeant Major Kevin Grady who last week was a private, his rapid promotion due to the discovery of his commanding officer's boots under his wife's bed; every night since he had looked under the bed for further promotion. All were converging on the church where Father Rudden now stood over four unconscious Ulster Police, while a fifth had escaped to the border post and was shouting insults.

'You can have 'em for ten pounds in the poor box,'

was the priest's reply, at which moment MacGilli-kudie and Co, both brakes and all hope gone, shot into the churchyard and hit a tombstone. All three were catapulted up through the stained glass window. Ah Pong fell unconscious on the organ keyboard and a mighty atonal chord ensued. Milligan and the Sergeant were hurtled into the middle of the organ pipes, which began to fall like iron rain, clanging into the empty aisle.

Outside the militia truck drew up with a screech and out shot a crowd in mixed uniforms who immediately threw a cordon round each other. Guffaws came from troops at the Customs post. Enraged Sergeant Grady barked, 'Take aim, one round over dem laffin bastards' heads – fire!' To the accompaniment of clanging organ pipes a volley rent the air.

'Caw!' said a crow.

'Help!' said the Milligan, an organ pipe jammed over his head.

A return volley from the Customs post whistled overhead, a bullet hit Milligan's pipe, and vibrations of 300 decibels in E flat didn't help his temper. Soon, volleys of 'over the head fire' from both sides were all the rage. Father Rudden ran up and down his line of Ulster police, hitting each one as he became conscious. Smoke bombs were being thrown.

'Look out!' yelled a voice.

Into their midst galloped a horse desperately trying to keep up with the cage it was pulling; through the middle it plunged, scattering them all, flattening the Customs shed, trampling tents. The coffin in the shed burst into flames. At 4.32 the world of Puckoon erupted in a crimson-throated roar, with screams, smoke, yells, swears; debris flew everywhere, the clock in the church suddenly struck endless ones, hundreds of bats flew from their belfry; one hundred and fifty feet up, Ah Pong regained consciousness and blew his whistle. Father Rudden was blown backwards out of his boots. MacGillikudie's moustache was singed from his face, he hid his shame with a bucket over his head. The great bell fell from the tower and landed directly over Mr Prells. The nights are closing in he thought. The dust and debris settled. A great silence settled over the land. Ten years have passed since that fateful day, ten years have journeyed to their end and Puckoon once again was lost in its unhurried ways. The Church was restored by a rich Catholic, Father Rudden found faith in a pair of new boots. The mute steeple clock once again ticked out with a new life, the border posts were never rebuilt, to this very day no one is quite sure exactly where the border lies, in fact each and every character in the picture returned to his or her own ways, all except one man, a Roman Soldier hanging from a tree with a rusty organ pipe lodged over his head, from where came a muffled voice. 'You can't leave me like this!'

'Oh, can't I?'

More about Penguins

Penguinews, which appears every month,
contains details of all the new books issued by
Penguins as they are published. From time to time
it is supplemented by *Penguins in Print*, which is a
complete list of all books published by Penguins
which are in print. (There are well over four
thousand of these.)

A specimen copy of *Penguinews* will be
sent to you free on request. For a year's issues
(including the complete lists) send 30p if you
live in the United Kingdom, or 60p if you
live elsewhere. Just write to Dept EP, Penguin
Books Ltd, Harmondsworth, Middlesex,
enclosing a cheque or postal order, and your name
will be added to the mailing list.

Note *Penguinews* and *Penguins in Print*
are not available in the U.S.A. or Canada

Also by Spike Milligan

Small Dreams of a Scorpion

They chop down 100ft trees
To make chairs
I bought one
I am six-foot one inch
When I sit in the chair
I'm four foot two.
Did they really chop down a 100ft tree
To make me look shorter?

Here's a volume of Millipoems on pollution,
population and conservation – serious subjects,
overlaid by the inimitable Milligan humour.

Adolf Hitler – My Part in His Downfall

'*At Victoria Station the R.T.O. gave me a travel warrant,
a white feather and a picture of Hitler marked "This is
your enemy". I searched every compartment but he wasn't on
the train . . .*'

Spike Milligan's on the march, blitzing friend and
foe alike with his uproarious recollections of army life
from enlistment to the landing at Algiers in 1943.
Bathos, pathos, gales of drunken laughter, and
insane military goonery explode in superlative
Milliganese.

'It is the most irreverent, hilarious book about the
war that I have ever read' – *Sunday Express*

Not for Sale in the U.S.A.